SCRATCH

by Archibald MacLeish

A New Play suggested by Stephen Vincent Benet's
short story, "The Devil and Daniel Webster"

Originally produced on the Broadway Stage by
Stuart Ostrow

THE DRAMATIC PUBLISHING COMPANY

CHICAGO

Archibald Mac Leish

Awarded one Pulitzer prize for playwrighting, and two Pulitzer prizes for poetry.

Bollington Prize for Poetry

Boston Arts Festival Poetry Award

National Book Award

Assistant Secretary of State

Librarian of Congress

Boylston Professor at Harvard

Chairman of the American Delegation to the U.N. Conferences which founded UNESCO

The most recent work by Archibald MacLeish is the play SCRATCH.

ST. JAMES THEATER

STUART OSTROW

presents

SCRATCH

by

Archibald MacLeish

A New Play suggested by Stephen Vincent Benet's
short story, "The Devil and Daniel Webster"

Scenery by **JOHN CONKLIN**

Costumes by **PATRICIA ZIPPRODT**

Lighting by **FEDER**

Hair Styles by Ernest Adler

Makeup by Joseph Cranzano

Directed by

Peter H. Hunt

Starring

PATRICK MAGEE
WILL GEER
ROY POOLE
WILL MACKENZIE

with

REX ROBBINS	PHILIP CARLING	JOANNE NAIL
DINO LAUDICINA	WALTER GORNEY	THOMAS BARBOUR
WILLIAM FRANCIS	MARY LOANE	JOHN COE
DANIEL KEYES	DOMINIC CHIANESE	PETER HARRIS
ROBERT BAINES	RICHARD HAMILTON	GARNETT SMITH

Original Cast Recording — Caedmon Records

SCRATCH

A New Play

Six Principal Roles and Nineteen Small Parts
(Twelve Small Parts, with Doubling*)

CHARACTERS

DANIEL WEBSTER
SCRATCH
JABEZ STONE
WESTON . . . . *a Massachusetts farmer*
SETH PETERSON ⎤
PORTER WRIGHT │
TOM │
GARNETT │ . . . . *the hired men*
JOHN │
ROBERT ⎦
MRS. WESTON ⎤
THE HIRED GIRL ⎦ . . .*the women of the household*
JUDGE ⎤ . . . . *figures out of the past*
JURY ⎦
VOICE. . . . . *offstage*

PLACE: *New England*
TIME: *Summer, 1850*

* The men in Scene Two may double as members
of the jury in Scene Four. Two of the small parts
are for women; they also may double as members
of the jury.

Prologue

An empty, New England barn cluttered with old
furniture, discarded farm machinery and a
casual collection of the relics and mementoes
of the first century of the Republic--an old
flag, a bust of General Washington, the figurehead of a ship. A shaft of early morning sunlight streams from a pane of glass above the
huge barn door. JABEZ STONE, a youngish
man in the business uniform of the decade before
the Civil War, stands looking up at it. To his
left, white head dozing on a chair, is what
might be a statue of DANIEL WEBSTER in the
famous blue coat and canary waistcoat. To
JABEZ' right, slumped in a second chair, is a
second, but very different, white-headed figure
in a flowery vest, with a great incongruous
sack over his shoulder. This is SCRATCH.

JABEZ (looking at the shaft of light, turning speaking to the audience). It's morning. . . . (Pause.)
I'm still here. (Silence. He turns to the
figure at his left.) Mr. Webster! (Louder.)
Mr. Webster! (WEBSTER stirs.) It is! It's
morning!
WEBSTER. Good Morning, Jabez. (WEBSTER
rises, plunges his arms into the shaft of sun.)
SCRATCH (rousing in his turn, groaning, stretching).
Morning! Whoever heard of welcoming a
morning? Beastliest moment of the blasted

7

day! The blinding light! Night's the time to
wait for in this filthy world--the evening's dim
refusal--the denying dark.

JABEZ (to the audience). Mr. Webster loves the
mornings. The Devil . . . (A gesture toward
SCRATCH.) . . . don't. And there are other
things they can't agree on. The greatest law
case ever argued in the country--it never got
written down in the books, but the greatest law
case--was tried between them once in this same
barn.

WEBSTER. Nip and tuck . . .

SCRATCH. And no holds barred! (The two bow to
each other, WEBSTER in the shaft of sunlight.)

(A sharp, brisk, brassy bell. We think at first it
might be a ringside signal--but then it goes
clanging on and on and we know what it is: an
old-fashioned call to breakfast. We are in:)

Scene 1

The kitchen at Marshfield at dawn on a July day in
1850. Lantern light. Huge table. Coffee pot
as big as a milk pail, cream in great pint
pitchers, mountains of butter, bowls of summer
flowers. The HIRED GIRL, buxom and crisp
as a trayful of laundry, circles the table with
last-minute spoons, plates, napkins, cups.
MRS. WESTON, arms under her apron, surveys
the scene from the door to the summer kitchen.
[During this scene, she appears and disappears
as she goes about her work.]

Scraping and stamping of barnyard boots. WESTON
comes in with WRIGHT and the rest of the
HIRED MEN.

TOM. Morning, ma'am.
GARNETT. Bid ye good morning, Mrs. Weston.
JOHN. Fresh bread this morning: I can smell it.
WRIGHT. Good morning, ma'am. I'll have my
usual beefsteak. Fried.
MRS. WESTON. You will if I happen to think of it,
Porter.
ROBERT. Popovers! As I live and breathe, pop-
overs!
WESTON. I'll stick to poi. There's blueberry poi
this morning. Susan told me--didn't you,
Susan?
HIRED GIRL. I never, Mrs. Weston!
MRS. WESTON. What would it matter, child?
There is. (She withdraws.)

(A great scraping of chair legs on the floor; clatter
of plates, knives, spoons; cream pitchers go
sailing back and forth from hand to hand; the

9

HIRED GIRL swings round the table with platters of steak, eggs, bacon, pie--and all the
while the big pine chair at the head of the table
stands magnificently empty. A tuneless voice
off. WEBSTER appears.)

WEBSTER. Ah, the mornings! the mornings! (He
takes his seat in the noble old Windsor chair,
shakes out his napkin with a flourish; disappears
behind the HIRED GIRL pouring his coffee,
serving his butter, passing him popovers;
emerges again.)

WESTON. Never miss a morning, do you, Mr.
Webster?

WEBSTER. Good morning, Mrs. Weston! Good
morning! Magnificent popovers! You remember how I love them.

MRS. WESTON (off). I remember how you eat
them, anyway.

(MRS. WESTON appears in the doorway.)

MRS. WESTON. Good morning. We're happy to
have you home. (She is out again.)

WEBSTER. And I'm happy to be here. You've no
idea how happy. (To WESTON.) No, I never
miss a sunrise here at Marshfield. Coffee,
Porter, please.

(PETERSON enters, crosses, head down, to the
foot of the table.)

WEBSTER. Good morning, Seth: haven't seen you
since December, have I? Day we walked down
to the river at dawn with the tide in and the
marshes covered and not a breath of wind on
the water anywhere--ice-blue and the port

deserted, the lobster houses boarded up--only
the Canada geese on the still river and, out
against the sun, wild swans. Remember that?
(PETERSON sits and doesn't answer. WEBSTER,
momentarily puzzled, turns back to WESTON.)
No, never miss them here and not often in
Washington. I know the morning. I am
acquainted with it and I love it, fresh and sweet
as it is, a daily new creation breaking forth.
(The GIRL swings around again.) Pie? I don't
care if I do. Just a bit of it--a quarter, maybe.
They look like low-bush blueberries. Nature's
greatest gift to New England. Next to the bluefish, Seth, of course.

WRIGHT (sourly, a sidewise look down the table to
PETERSON). Next to the Yankees!

WEBSTER (to WRIGHT). Well, the country Yankees
maybe: not the Bostonians. They never see
the sun rise in their lives.

WESTON. Except in winter when it rises 'long
toward noon.

WRIGHT. Nor the nights either with those street
lights they keep blazing, dusk to dawn.

WEBSTER. Oh, the nights! Who cares about the
nights? Night is a wilderness you're meant to
sleep through the way you sleep through pine
scrub on the cars . . . so long, that is, as
you don't dream. I dreamt last night. First
time in a dog's age. I dreamt . . . something
or someone leaned so close above me I could
hear its . . . heart. Enormous heart beats
. . . I was terrified . . . I couldn't move--
breathe even. (Pause, silence.) I seemed to
know, the way you do in dreams, that what was
standing--leaning over me--was . . . evil.
Not just bad or frightening but evil. Evil! The
way the stench of death is death. I knew what

it was, of course . . . when I woke up.

PETERSON (under his breath). The Devil stalking
  you.

WRIGHT (to PETERSON). For God's sake, don't
  start that again.

PETERSON. They say his heart beats something
  awful when he gets you down.

WESTON (to WEBSTER). Of course you knew what
  it was. The sea. The rut of the sea on the
  north beach.

WEBSTER. Rut of the sea. I've heard it often
  enough when the wind drops after a blow like
  yesterday's. There's a word for Mr. Peterson
  to remember. Rut. Latin *rota* meaning rep-
  etition. Too slow for a heart, of course, but
  in a dream . . .

PETERSON. Not too slow for his heart. They say
  it beats the way a turtle's . . .

(MRS. WESTON appears beyond the table.)

WEBSTER (to PETERSON). What's this you're
  saying--or not saying?

PETERSON (back to his steak). Nothing. . . .
  (Looking up at WEBSTER: a slow look.) I've
  been reading, that's all. In the papers.

MRS. WESTON (taking charge, throwing the helm
  sharp over). I suppose you'll be leaving us
  quick as you came, Mr. Webster, now you're
  in the Cabinet again.

WEBSTER. Drat the Cabinet! The only Cabinet I
  want a part of is your husband and Porter
  Wright and this seagoing Satanist, Seth. We've
  done more State Department business here in
  Marshfield than anyone in Washington ever
  guessed. Maybe some of you recall my nego-
  tiations with the British when I was Secretary

of State before. I settled every question of
magnitude in the Washington discussions except one and that was the most important
question of all--fishing rights. (This is the
expansive moment after breakfast: he leans
back, talking for the pleasure of it, the men
at ease in their chairs, the girl and MRS.
WESTON beyond.) That topic I reserved to
take up with Mr. Peterson here, on Ned's
Ground, off Bluefish Rock, at six on a Sep-
tember morning--a warm, still, smoky day,
the wind southeast and a swell running.

PETERSON. Mostly halibut, as I recall--one or
two quite sizable.

WEBSTER (a slow, rich laugh). It was there, on
that occasion, that Mr. Peterson delivered
himself of the great political principle which
has guided my efforts ever since. "There is
sometimes," said Seth, "an odd fish too smart
to take the bait. You must try him with the
naked hook. The smarter he is the quicker
he'll swallow it."

PETERSON. Have it your own way, Mr. Webster.
It wasn't political principles we were talking
about; it was President Tyler's troubles. I
said the fault was in the Congress. They ought
to take hold, man-fashion, and do up the public
business. Mr. Tyler was not to blame for
being President: if President Harrison hadn't
died he never would have been, and nobody
better pleased than himself. He understood
what it was to be Vice-President and he liked it.
A Vice-President, he knew, is like a cod: a
bottom feeder--never ought to be seen at the
surface. Mr. Tyler liked that kind of job.

WEBSTER. As every Senator likes it: bottom
feeders to the last man!

PETERSON. Ha! Senators! More like marlin.
    Dancing around on their tails to show they're
    there.
WEBSTER. But you like marlin, Seth. You know
    you like them. You'll let a blue go any day to
    watch the marlin leap.
PETERSON. Oh, yes, to watch them break. But
    not with the hook in the mouth, Mr. Webster.
    Not when they try to throw the hook. That, I
    don't care to look at.

(MRS. WESTON, who had gone back into the summer
    kitchen, appears again, her hands under her
    apron.)

PETERSON. That's for those tiptoe fish, all flash
    and splash and not worth having when you take
    them. The really big ones stay below. And
    pull. Like horses. Nothing can get them up
    until their hearts break. They don't . . . quit!
WRIGHT (to SETH). Seth, I thought we had agreed.
WEBSTER. Careful what you say of senators,
    Peterson. I was a Senator myself last week.
MRS. WESTON. And for some weeks before that.
WESTON. Not to say years.
MRS. WESTON. Long as anyone in this house can
    remember.
PETERSON. Good one, too.
WRIGHT. Good! There was never better. Calhoun
    and Clay were minnows to him! Fry fish!
WEBSTER. Don't bully him, Porter. Good, in
    Seth's vocabulary, means what it says. I'm
    grateful for it.
WRIGHT. I suppose you're grateful for the rest of
    it, too!
WEBSTER. The rest of it?
WRIGHT. The Devil getting you down: getting the

best of you.

WESTON. That's enough, Wright.

PETERSON. You ought to read the papers, Porter. It wasn't me who tossed the Devil into Mr. Webster's dream. Every respected writer in the Commonwealth has had his say about it since that speech of Mr. Webster's four months ago. Seventh March, Eighteen-fifty! They know that date, every one of them.

WRIGHT. You stop him, Weston? All day long . . .

PETERSON. Even Mister Greenleaf Whittier, that old, bald, blatting, bleating sheep!

WEBSTER. Seth! Seth! Don't let them make you angry.

PETERSON. They ought to make you angry, Daniel. You know what Mr. Whittier says? "When faith is lost, when honor dies, the man is dead." That's you, he means. He called his poem "Ichabod"--any Yankee knows what "Ichabod" intends to say. It's in First Samuel: "The Glory is departed." (Pause.) Your glory, Daniel. . . . Ours . . .

WEBSTER. All right, Seth, but don't get angry. Not with them. With me if you have to: not with them. Times like these turn men to bigots. Right becomes absolute right and wrong absolute wrong. Even your most amiable friend will mount upon his sense of duty as upon a war horse and go galloping off over every other man and every other duty that stands in his way. What would be differences of opinion at any other time become, at a time like this, differences between good and evil, between Heaven and Hell.

PETERSON. But there are differences between Heaven and Hell, Daniel, and there is right and there is wrong, and every now and again a

duty does turn up that you have to mount and
ride like a war horse. (Pause: PETERSON
gets control of himself.) Why did you have to
say it, Daniel? In the Senate . . .

WEBSTER. I said a number of things in the Senate.
I said there were grievances on both sides,
North and South, and men exploiting those
grievances on both sides, exaggerating them.

PETERSON. About the law.

WEBSTER. I said the law must be enforced.

PETERSON. You said the Fugitive Slave Law must
be enforced.

WRIGHT. No! I won't sit here and . . . (Chairs
are pushed back, voices break in--and MRS.
WESTON, all sails set, comes wheeling 'round
the table.)

WEBSTER. You will sit here!

MRS. WESTON. Excuse me, Mr. Webster, but he
won't. Nor the rest of you, neither. This is
not the Senate. This is an honest woman's
kitchen, with dishes to wash for seven men and
a floor to mop after muddy boots and a lamb
stew to start for a twelve o'clock dinner and . . .

WESTON. Not to speak of a day's work to be
planned . . .

WEBSTER. Very well. Very well. Give us a moment, Mrs. Weston, and Seth and I will have it
out. With blunt words. At four feet. But first,
the day . . . (WEBSTER and WESTON hit the
words together:)

WEBSTER and WESTON. Proverbs XXVIII, verse
23. "Be diligent to know the state of thy flocks
--(All join in.)--and look well to thy herds."
(The laughter of relief.)

WEBSTER. Specifically, take the oxen to the beach
for kelp. Never forget, it was fish, kelp and
barn-manure made Marshfield what it is: Work

it in! Work it in! Don't mind the ladies. Tell
'em it's Marshfield roses they smell.

WESTON. We'll tell the ladies you say so, Mr.
Secretary.

WEBSTER. What else?

WRIGHT. Your horses, Mr. Webster.

WEBSTER. Ah, yes, my roans. Liberty and
Union. Best we've ever seen at Marshfield or
anywhere else in the Commonwealth. (Pause.)
Well, we all get older . . . get old. At least
they went together. Sad, though . . . (Silence.)

WRIGHT. They ought to be buried before--well,
the sun gets <u>too</u> high.

WEBSTER. But bury them with all the honors of
war. Bury them standing side by side in the
same grave with their shoes on and their hal-
ters buckled. Choose a site by the sea where
you can hear the sound. A slate stone. Black,
not gray. With an inscription . . .

WESTON. We thought we'd use those words of
yours every schoolboy knows: "Liberty and
Union, now and forever, one and inseparable."

PETERSON. You won't get 'em side by side in the
same grave if you do. Not now. Not any more.
Not since that speech of the seventh March.
Union comes first and Liberty afterward these
days. <u>Way</u> afterward! So far after, you'll
have to bury them nose to tail. Liberty's nose
to Union's tail . . .

WRIGHT. Can't you let up on it even for one . . .

WEBSTER. All right, Seth: we'll talk about it--
try to. As for the rest of you, dig the grave,
get the kelp in, dress the pasture . . . (WES-
TON turns to go, the others following.) . . .
Oh, and about that epitaph. We'll change it.
Not so much in respect for Mr. Peterson's
emotions as in respect for the roans. They

deserve the durability of Latin.   Chalk <u>this</u> on
your slate and cut it later:

> *Siste Viator!*
> *Viator te major hic sistet.*

Which I take to mean--Seth will correct me--
he's been talking Latin all through breakfast----

> *Wait traveler!*
> *A greater traveler than you waits here.*

Appropriate, don't you think, Mr. Peterson?
We're all travelers in this place--though we
don't know yet from where to where.

> *Siste Viator!*

(WESTON and his men crowd out the door.
WEBSTER calls over his shoulder to the summer
kitchen.) Magnificent breakfast, Mrs. Weston.
As always. Except for the maple syrup, and
that was the best in seven years. (Pause. No
answer. WEBSTER turns to PETERSON who
sits in a dogged Yankee silence, head down.)
It's true, too. This was a great year for maple,
Mr. Weston tells me. Fine, cold nights in
February: sun-thaws at noon. Sugar weather.
(No response from PETERSON.) It's the
weather, not the calendar, that counts. Remember that sensible Latin advice to farmers
--plow naked and sow naked? You know what
that means.

PETERSON (head still down). Means you shouldn't
crowd the season. No use calling it spring till

it warms up.

WEBSTER. That's good advice still, Mr. Peterson.
Wait till you know where you are before you lay
about you. And don't just take the season from
the books. Our ancestors used to plant corn by
the almanac: May first, Old Style; May elev-
enth, New. The Indians knew better. They put
their corn in the ground when the new leaf on
the white oak was as big as a mouse's ear.
Years vary.

PETERSON. Don't tell that to me, Mr. Webster.
Tell it to the men who write the books. Mr.
Greenleaf Whittier. Dr. Oliver Wendell Holmes.
Mr. Emerson. Mr. Thoreau. I just read. I'm
the hired man. Authority on . . . barn-manure
. . . horse-shit . . .

WEBSTER. Trout. Woodcock. Black duck. Not
to mention halibut, cod, blues.

PETERSON. And horse-shit. Don't leave out the
horse-shit. That's what you think, so say it!

WEBSTER. I think when you talk about that speech
of mine and ask me why I urged the enforcement of the law . . .

PETERSON (jerking his head up at last). Of the
Fugitive Slave Law!

WEBSTER. . . . you don't know what you're talking about. The Constitution of the United States
enjoins the enforcement of such laws. Persons
held to service in one state and escaping into
another must be returned to servitude.

PETERSON. Which is why the abolitionists down in
Boston call the Constitution an agreement with
Hell and a covenant with death.

WEBSTER. Abolitionists! Your abolitionist is one
of those who ride the blind horse of ungovern-
able duty. He knows his right is right and
everyone else's right is wrong and he proposes

that his right shall triumph even if it brings
the country down. Covenant with death! Does
it ever cross his righteous mind to count the
thousands upon thousands of young men, North
as well as South and South as well as North,
who'd die if once his Covenant with Death were
abrogated? Think of the Union, Seth! Think
what would happen to the Union--to the Country
--the Republic!

PETERSON (his voice low, almost gentle). And
you, Daniel. Think of the slaves! Think what
has happened to the slaves! (Pause.) And to
their masters! . . . (Pause.) And to us who
share this continent with their masters! . . .

WEBSTER. Precisely! To us who share this continent with their masters! Oh, I wish I could
make you see it, Seth. The Constitution, like
everything else in life, like life itself, is a
compromise. I've told you again and again: All
legislation, all government, all society, is
formed upon the principle of mutual concessions,
politeness, comity, courtesy.

PETERSON. So are all lies, all cheats, all . . .
(Fumbling for the words.) . . . degrading ar-
rangements. Don't you see, Daniel, why they
bring the Devil into it? Why they say you've
yielded to the Tempter? They mean just that.
They mean you've compromised--and compromise in these parts is where the Devil gets his
thumb in and the girl rolls over.

WEBSTER. Compromised! Of course we've compromised. We compromised in Missouri. We
compromised in South Carolina. We've been
compromising for a generation because, for a
generation, secession has been a possibility,
and secession means civil war.

PETERSON. But they mean you. You, Daniel!

They mean you've compromised. Here's Dr.
Holmes. He calls it . . . (Fishing in his over-
all pocket, pulling out a clipping.) . . . "The
Statesman's Secret." He even knows the bait
the Tempter's offered you. . . .

WEBSTER. Bait!

PETERSON. The presidency.

WEBSTER. Fairly open secret! There isn't a
four-year-old in Massachusetts doesn't know I
want the presidency. It is the greatest office
in the world and I am but a man, sir. I want it.
I want it! And I hope to have it even now. Is
that the end of it?

PETERSON. Of Dr. Holmes, yes.

WEBSTER. Who else bears witness?

PETERSON. Mr. Emerson. (WEBSTER's face
tightens: pause.)

WEBSTER. Well, are you going to let me hear
it?

PETERSON (gently). If you wish to hear it.

"Why did all manly gifts in Webster fail?
He wrote on Nature's grandest brow, For Sale!"

(Silence; WEBSTER staring into PETERSON's
face, not seeing it.) That's what they're saying, Daniel. . . . Forgive me for . . . know-
ing it.

WEBSTER. For sale! My opinions, my beliefs,
for sale! What right has Mr. Emerson to say
so? What act of mine would justify such--cal-
umny?

PETERSON. Are you asking me?

WEBSTER. In Mr. Emerson's absence.

PETERSON. He means that speech.

WEBSTER. That I offered, in that speech, to sell
my principles for the presidency?

PETERSON. More or less.

WEBSTER. Is that what <u>you</u> think, Seth? Is that
  what you've been saying? Or not saying?

PETERSON. I've fished with you too often, Daniel.
  I know how you stay with . . . your convictions.

WEBSTER. That's not good enough.

PETERSON. No, it's not good enough. You've
  never let up on a fish to my knowledge but in
  that speech . . .

WEBSTER. I let up on slavery?

PETERSON. Put it that you . . . changed your
  mind.

WEBSTER. And you want to know why? . . . You
  and Mr. Emerson.

PETERSON. Mr. Emerson seems to know already.

WEBSTER. Yes: not even God can tell Mr.
  Emerson. But maybe Daniel Webster can tell
  you. (Pause.) I tried to say it in the Senate
  when I rose that day to speak. "Mr. President,"
  I said, "I wish to speak to you today not as a
  Massachusetts man, nor as a Northern man,
  but as an American, a member of the Senate
  of the United States. I speak today for the preservation of the Union. (Pause.) Hear me for
  my cause. (Pause.) Hear . . . "

PETERSON (brusquely). I know the speech! (Silence.)

WEBSTER. Look, Seth. I want you to see something. A bright day--bright morning. March
  is often fine in Washington. Not like the
  blasted season here--the late sleet. We are in
  the Senate chamber--sunlight--the room full
  --not only the senators' desks and the galleries
  but the whole room: visitors everywhere--
  women, mostly--hats like flowers in the sun--
  lovely dresses. They are perched on senators'
  chairs, on the steps to the Vice-President's

seat--everywhere. The great room is fragrant with them. . . .(Pause.) Walker of Wisconsin has the floor--he was speaking when we adjourned yesterday--but he yields to me. (Pause.) I had waited seven days to speak. I suppose I was nearly broken down with anxiety and waiting and the words of the Old President, John Quincy Adams, were ringing in my ears. He'd told me in 'Forty-eight, before he died, that he'd give the Union five years more and the years were running out. I stood there looking at the sunlight on the dresses and counting the years. California was about to enter the Union as free soil--and New Mexico was certain to enter the Union as free soil and Oregon would follow them in; and if California and New Mexico and the rest entered the Union as free soil, the slave states would go out. They had already called a convention to meet in Nashville, in June. (He strikes his fist into his hand.) In Nashville! Over the bones of Andrew Jackson! (He lifts his head.) If the slave states went out it meant war. (Pause.) I stood there counting the years on my fingers. (Silence.) You asked me why I had to say what I said. I saw in the flooding sunlight in that crowded room, among the pretty hats and lifted faces, the Union shattered . . . and the stain of blood. (Silence.) You tell me I have changed my mind. You seem to say I have changed my mind about slavery. I have not changed my mind about slavery. I detest slavery. I regard slavery as a great moral and political evil, a degraded and degrading evil, degrading to master as to slave, more degrading to master than to slave. . . . I abhor slavery!

PETERSON (speaking with difficulty). I know. You

couldn't change your mind about slavery any
more than a cow could change her mind about
thistles. But you have changed, Daniel. You've
changed about . . . the Union.

WEBSTER. The Union! I love the Union! The whole
of my public life has been devoted to the preservation of the Union. Years I should have spent
at the Supreme Court bar arguing famous cases
for fat fees to keep my wife in silks and Marshfield solvent I spent on the Senate floor instead,
in Senate Committees, cloakrooms, boarding-
houses, wearing the carpets threadbare for my
single cause. I could have been a rich man,
Seth: not, as I am, half bankrupt and dependent
on the contributions of my constituents.   But,
oh, my friend . . . (His hand on SETH's sleeve.)
I love the Union.

PETERSON. I know you do. Maybe that's what I'm
saying, Daniel. People can change about a
thing by loving it as easy as by hating it.   A
woman who loves her house can come to love it,
not for her husband's comfort or her children's
joy, but for itself--order and neatness for the
sake of order and neatness. You know what that
does to a family. The same thing can happen
with a country--with a man and his country--with
you and the Union. You love the Union: you
always have. But once you loved it for the kind
of life a man could live in it--a free life. Now
you love it for itself. Because it's powerful.
Because it's rich. (The cud is too bitter for
PETERSON to swallow.) Maybe you'll even
come to love it for its slavery--because it's
rich in slaves. (WEBSTER wheels on him,
black with rage.) No, hear me, Daniel! Hear
me . . . for my cause. It's not your hatred of
slavery which has changed. It's the way you

love the Union--what you think of when you say you love the Union. Once you thought of men-- free men . . .

WEBSTER. Will you let me say for myself what I think of when I name the Union? I think of the failure and chaos and misery under the old Confederation of States into which I was born. I think of the prosperity and power of the new Union of the States, its flag on every sea, its frontiers on the coasts of a vast continent. I think of the mortal danger that all our hopes, all our prospects of greatness, may collapse in war. It is of this I think--all this--when I name the Union. And when I think of this, all this, I swear to Almighty God that the Union shall not fail: that the preservation of the Union shall come first . . .

PETERSON. First? . . .

WEBSTER. Before everything!

PETERSON. Before human liberty?

WEBSTER. Human liberty! Human liberty! People talked about human liberty in the old Confeder- ation. They ranted against the Constitution in the name of human liberty. And how much hu- man liberty did they have? Just about enough to want for everything--to hunger--to quarrel, state against state--to be miserable. What's human liberty without a country?

PETERSON. Or a country . . . without human liberty?

WEBSTER. All this . . . all this is ghostly ab- straction! Ghostly abstraction! The Union is real. It exists . . . trades . . . traffics . . . builds . . . expands . . .

PETERSON. And liberty isn't real? Is that what you're saying?

WEBSTER. Not until you make it real. Not until

you give it a country . . . a people. There has
to be a country first before there's freedom in
a country. And a country's difficult, Seth: It
takes work to make it--time--patience--intelli-
gence--good will. Generations have to give
their lives to it. You know that. Think of the
great men, living and dead, who gave their
lives, their blood, their hope, to make this
country. Think of that before you tear it down
to right a wrong . . . however grievous.
(PETERSON sits silent, staring at his hands.)
Think of the Union, Seth--how she stands there!
(Silence.)

PETERSON. I'm thinking of her, Daniel. But all I
seem to see is . . . men. Black men. White
men. Oh, men aren't much, I grant you. Men
will lie, kill, fornicate like rabbits, follow
each other's follies like so many sheep. Still,
they're men. They matter.

WEBSTER. They matter with a government to gov-
ern them. Freedom under government. Without
it they're . . . a mob! I've seen mobs, Mr.
Peterson.

PETERSON. And I've seen men, and maybe that's
the difference! (PETERSON starts out, turns,
pauses behind WEBSTER. A gesture of affec-
tion.) I love the Union dear as you do, Daniel
. . . (WEBSTER stirs.) . . . well, almost
. . . but not for itself. I love it for its men.
(Silence, WEBSTER staring into the dark.) I
suppose a statesman has to count by govern-
ments but a Yankee don't: he counts by heads,
by people. (Straightening up to go.) You're a
Yankee, Daniel. Count by men and . . . shame
the Devil. (He goes out.)

(The light fades. We are in:)

Scene 2

Webster's back yard at Marshfield. High noon.
    WEBSTER drowsing in his chair under the
    gigantic elms. Flickering light and shade.
    SCRATCH appears out of shadow into sun.

SCRATCH. Mr. Webster? . . . (WEBSTER lifts
    his heavy head, peers around him in the dazzle,
    misses SCRATCH, then sees him.)
WEBSTER. I am Daniel Webster. You, sir?
SCRATCH. You don't know me?
WEBSTER. Should I?
SCRATCH. Most men do . . . in your profession.
WEBSTER. Hardly a compliment to you. The kind
    of men most lawyers know . . .
SCRATCH. Did I mention lawyers, Mr. Webster?
    I apologize.
WEBSTER. Ah, of course--a politician. I should
    have known it by your . . . consummate ef-
    frontery. I was asleep, sir! . . . attempting,
    that is, to fall asleep.
SCRATCH. Attempting! Under the elm trees at
    the flood of noon and snoring like a double-
    ended saw!
WEBSTER. Your business, sir? You tell me you're
    a politician . . .
SCRATCH. I did not say so. You did. But the
    term will serve. I find myself at home with
    politicians. They speak my language. Con-
    stituents! They love to talk of their constitu-
    ents. So do I.
WEBSTER. And yours, of course, are numerous.
SCRATCH. Quite numerous. A clear majority.
WEBSTER. I'm sure. No politician worthy of the
    name claims less.
SCRATCH. And Daniel Webster is a politician

27

    worthy of the name. What majority does <u>he</u>
    claim?

WEBSTER (closing his eyes). None. I am a can-
    didate for nothing . . . but the arms of Morpheus.

SCRATCH. Candidate for nothing!

WEBSTER. Nothing.

SCRATCH. Not even for the Pres-i-den-cy?

WEBSTER. For no office!

SCRATCH. You are Daniel Webster, aren't you?
    (WEBSTER opens one eye.) But no, I have no
    need to ask. The whole world knows that head,
    that bearing. "Nature's . . . (The exagger-
    ated emphasis of quotation marks.) . . .
    grandest brow!"

WEBSTER (sitting up). I suggest, sir, it is time
    and more than time I knew your name.

SCRATCH. To think that I should meet you face to
    face! Secretary of State of the United States of
    America! Secretary for the second time!

WEBSTER. Your name! In three words, sir: Who
    are you?

SCRATCH. Oh, nothing as grand as Mr. Daniel
    Webster. There are some, like you, no office
    elevates because they are above all office: some,
    like me, no office seeks. Still, you have heard
    of me, I think--spoken of me, even.

WEBSTER. Spoken of you! Then there must have
    been a name to speak by.

SCRATCH. Scratch was your preference, I believe.
    Just Scratch. No honorific--nothing--just plain
    Scratch. Not much to boast of as a name, but
    still I have my little satisfactions--successes,
    even. Though none, I hasten to confess, was
    ever as spectacular as this--as fabulous--un-
    hoped for . . .

WEBSTER. <u>This</u>?

SCRATCH. This! I think you understand me.
(WEBSTER stares at him in blank silence.)
Have I been too credulous? (WEBSTER stares.)
There are always those who understand my
business better than I do myself and rush to
publicize my triumphs--I have long known that.
But these were reputable witnesses: writers
and the like of that--preachers--Boston preach-
ers--even a Concord philosopher. We take that
sort of testimony seriously where I come from.
Respectfully, you might say. And never has a
more remarkable consensus been recorded. So
I am told, and I believe it. They all agree.
WEBSTER. They all agree on what, sir? (SCRATCH
begins to walk through the elms, WEBSTER
following.)
SCRATCH. Why, that you have . . . seen the light.
Come 'round. Of course they use their own lo-
cutions: "yielded to the Tempter" is the ordinary phrase. But what they mean is clearly
that you've seen the light--reached the only
possible conclusion open to a realistic mind,
an honest intelligence. It makes me--you
could never guess how happy.
WEBSTER. Now just one moment . . .
SCRATCH. No, no: they're right. I quite agree with
them. You see, I've read your famous speech.
Magnificent achievement! That eloquent repu-
diation of your country's adolescent rhetoric--
the meretricious claptrap of its infant years--
that nonsense about "Liberty." Mankind en-
dowed by its . . . Creator . . . with certain
unalienable rights!
WEBSTER. Just: one: moment . . .
SCRATCH. "Unalienable rights!" What rights, I
ask you, has mankind? Mr. Jefferson seemed

to think it <u>wallowed</u> in them--at least he said
so in his <u>fatuous</u> Declaration.

WEBSTER. <u>One</u> <u>moment</u>!

SCRATCH. The <u>dignity</u> of man! The dignity of
<u>man</u>! Think of those mortal, momentary crea-
<u>tures</u>, half the weight and size of a sound calf,
strutting around the streets of Philadelphia in
horse dung talking of the dignity of man! The
<u>dignity</u>! I ask you! <u>Think</u> of it . . . Of <u>man</u>!
(He chokes with laughter, collapses into
Webster's chair.)

WEBSTER. Thank you. (SCRATCH waves a help-
less, apologetic hand at him.) And now, before this interesting conversation loses itself
in history altogether, or what you seem to
think is history, may I inquire once more <u>who</u>
you are? You say your name is Scratch.

SCRATCH (pulling himself together). No, no. They
<u>call</u> me Scratch. . . . (A grin.) As they called
<u>you</u>, when you were young, Black Dan. . . .
Your complexion, of course. Your father's
mother's family, as I recall it. The Batchelders.
One of those fine old swarthy British strains that
go 'way back before the Britons. Back of the
golden Gaels. The Picts. Back to the first be-
ginnings--lost beginnings in the prehistoric dark
where all the greatness comes from. The orig-
inals! I have family connections of my own in
those beginnings.

WEBSTER. Have you indeed!

SCRATCH. I have. <u>In</u> <u>deed</u>. I do not lie about my
genealogy. Or <u>anything</u> else, for the matter of
that. I tell the truth. Those who are not accus-
tomed to the truth--and they are numerous--
take it for falsehood sometimes. But you, of
course, are familiar with <u>that</u> phenomenon.

WEBSTER. Forgive me if I <u>seem</u> persistent. You

say they call you Scratch. You intimate we
know each other.

SCRATCH. Oh, yes. We know each other, Mr.
Webster.

WEBSTER. Scratch? I have never so much as
heard the name in these parts nor up in New
Hampshire, either, nor anywhere else in
New England. And I know New England. I
know New England better than most, I may
say. Never, anywhere, in all New England,
in sixty-eight years of unimpaired hearing
and a better than average interest in what's
being said to me--never have I heard of
Scratch. Oh, "the old Scratch," certainly,
but then . . .

SCRATCH. Then?

WEBSTER. It's not exactly what you'd call a
patronymic. I mean, there are no families
founded in those syllables. One talks of "the
old Scratch" in order not to speak of the unspeakable . . .

SCRATCH. You mean . . .

WEBSTER. The Devil . . . naturally.

SCRATCH. You make no difficulty with the term,
sir.

WEBSTER. Ah, you find the word offensive? I
withdraw it.

SCRATCH. Not in the least--not in the least offensive, Mr. Webster. No one likes to be
. . . unspeakable. Not even . . . (A slight
bow.) . . . I.

WEBSTER (staring at him). You ask me to believe . . .

SCRATCH. I do not ask you to believe anything.
Unlike some I can think of . . . (His glance
goes to the sky above the elms tops.) I never
ask anyone to believe. I find I have no need to.

WEBSTER. Then . . . you mean . . . (A cough
of astonished laughter.) . . . that's who you
are? (WEBSTER begins to laugh: a slow,
rich chuckle which goes out of control.) I
thought we'd lost you centuries ago back on
the other side in the old country fiddling
around at midnight by the beds of dying kings
and sick whores, and such-like prospects.
(Paroxysm of laughter.) Forgive me if I
seem uncivil but you . . . here! . . . (Wiping
his eyes.) The Devil in General Washington's
Republic!

SCRATCH. Where evil is of course unknown.

WEBSTER. Forgive me, sir: I see I go too far.
Let me put it this way: you'll find few prospects on this continent.

SCRATCH. Few, perhaps, but not the least or
worst. One I can think of has declared himself already. Four months and nineteen days
ago he told the Senate of your great Republic
that if forced to choose between the bright new
world of Mr. Jefferson and the realities of
what you . . . here . . . call . . . (Whipping
out a great red handkerchief and blowing an
ironic blast.) . . . life, he'd vote for life. Ah,
if he'd only known what life is, Mr. Webster.
What death is, I might add. But we will talk
of all that later. There will be time enough to
talk--well, not precisely time but . . .

WEBSTER. If your account of Eternity, sir, is no
more precise than your account of the Senate
of the United States, you will give me leave to
conclude that you have been in neither. I did
not choose between Mr. Jefferson's great dream
of liberty--his bright new world, as you so justly
call it--and the realities of politics. I did not

repudiate liberty!

SCRATCH. Quite right. Quite right. It was the
abolition of slavery you repudiated. (Another
blast on the great red handkerchief.) Slavery,
you pointed out, is in the Constitution. Oh,
not by name, not by name, but there. You
were recalling your country, as you have so
often, to the facts. You are a great champion
of the facts, Mr. Webster--the greatest champion of the facts the young republic has ever
had. Most of your countrymen prefer those
fine, inflated paperbags of rhetoric. "Pursuit
of happiness"! Who ever heard of the pursuit
of happiness? You know what greatness in a
country really is. Power! Not the gas bal-
loons of paper aspiration but the fact of power.
National power and the national prosperity
which is the means to power. Guns and gold.

WEBSTER. I cannot remember that I mentioned
either guns or gold . . . except to warn against
the guns.

SCRATCH. Nor New England textile mills--their
need for slave-grown cotton. Nor the need of
slave-grown cotton for New England mills.
And yet the Senate understood you and the
clamor stopped.

WEBSTER. I spoke for the preservation of the
Union.

SCRATCH. And you persuaded them: even though
it meant the preservation of something else as
well--something Mr. Jefferson's sacred Declaration promised to eradicate. Oh, you
were right. You were altogether right. You
were--you are--an honest man. You understand reality. (WEBSTER turns his back on
him.) Am I offensive? When a man so loves

the truth as you do, Mr. Webster, he should
welcome it in others. Particularly when it
sheds such honor on himself. I admire you,
Mr. Webster. More than that--I value you.
I am, as I am sure you know, a--shall I say
collector?--of humanity . . . (He draws from
an inside pocket of his coat a fat, yellow leather wallet, strokes it as he talks.) . . . ex-
amples of humanity. A fascinating hobby. You
have no notion what varieties exist--what un-
expected specimens. You, sir, I should take
to be a most remarkable find. Most remarkable. Not only in yourself, your scope, your
scale, your . . . yes, your grandeur--twice
the dimensions ordinarily reported--not only
in yourself but in your representative capacity
--the thing you . . . (Lifting the leather wallet to conceal a smile.) . . . the thing you
stand for. If one could number <u>you</u> in his collection he could very well assert he <u>had</u> your
country!

WEBSTER. I represent the Commonwealth of
Massachusetts--nothing more and nothing less.
But I am also, as a man, American and I love
my country. When the issue is the preservation of my country I speak out. That is the issue now: whether this nation shall survive or
perish.

SCRATCH. Ah, you <u>did</u> speak out: You <u>did</u> declare
the issue. That <u>was</u> your great achievement,
Mr. Webster--your magnificent achievement.
You and you only understand what your republic is: not a philosopher's model of the rights
of man, whatever <u>they</u> may be, but just a . . .
country--a political contraption like another.
And you <u>said</u> so. And, saying so, you brushed
those smoldering, red, incendiary words aside

like coals upon a carpet and so saved the house.
Ah, Mr. Webster, Mr. Webster, there is nothing such a man as you does not deserve. Nothing he should not expect. With confidence. I propose to see your expectations realized.

WEBSTER. You propose!

SCRATCH. Why not? I am indebted to you, Mr. Webster. (Pause.) Or do you mean you doubt my influence in such matters?

WEBSTER. In what matters?

SCRATCH. Oh, the Baltimore Convention of your party.

WEBSTER. If your are what you say your are, you'll run the Baltimore Convention!

SCRATCH. Precisely. And the nomination will be yours.

WEBSTER. You make a dubious assumption.

SCRATCH. What assumption?

WEBSTER. That I want the nomination to that office . . .

SCRATCH. Mr. Webster!

WEBSTER. . . . at your hands.

SCRATCH. You must not be contemptuous, Mr. President. I offer you my help, no more. I ask for nothing.

WEBSTER. There is a proverb--I take it you don't care for proverbs--but you'll bear with just this one.

SCRATCH. It depends upon the proverb.

WEBSTER. "When the Old Scratch asks for nothing . . ."

SCRATCH. Nothing not already given . . .

WEBSTER. That's not the proverb. "When the Old Scratch asks for nothing, pat your pockets: you've been robbed."

SCRATCH. And that's the answer to the proverb: you gave it me yourself. You've . . . joined

me, Mr. Webster. Four months and nineteen
days ago. All New England is agreed on that
--the most intelligent Bostonians, and nothing
in Heaven or Earth--or elsewhere--is more
intelligent than a Bostonian. (WEBSTER rounds
on him: black angry brows: stares in silence.)
Perhaps you do not follow me.

WEBSTER. I trust I do not follow you . . .

SCRATCH. Why, then . . . you do!

WEBSTER (backing him toward the door). Because, if I were certain that I truly understood
you, I'd fling you headlong out the door, wit over
watchchain with your boots to follow. Call yourself what you please--Old Scratch--the Prince
of Darkness . . .

SCRATCH. Please, no poetry! I can't abide it!
(He pulls out the fat, yellow wallet.)

WEBSTER. And put that wallet in your pocket!
There's something crawling on it. What are
they--roaches?

SCRATCH. Some have thought so . . . some still
do. The Greeks decided they were moths, or
like moths--butterflies, probably. (Pause,
SCRATCH examining the wallet.) Psyche, you
remember, was the Attic term.

WEBSTER. Psyche! The soul? You don't pretend . . .

SCRATCH. Precisely. I do not pretend.

WEBSTER. . . . those are human souls you have.

SCRATCH. "Collected" is the word I use myself.

WEBSTER. . . . not here, though. Not in
Massachusetts.

SCRATCH. Too small, you think? No, no, quite
up to standard. Not your standard, naturally.
Not, at least, when you attain the presidency.
How does Dr. Holmes express it? "Build thee
more stately mansions, O my soul." Perhaps

he hasn't said it yet but when you fill the
White House . . .

WEBSTER. I make no question of their size but
of their origin. Even the Devil out of Hell
himself could take no souls in these United
States. No American would sell his soul.

SCRATCH. Ah? Because your country's new, you
trust the goodness of the Universe? Well . . .
(He snaps the wallet shut and crams it into his
pocket.) . . . others have trusted it before you,
Mr. Webster.

WEBSTER. Perhaps, but not my fellow countrymen. We believe in goodness but we trust
ourselves. My father, when he raised his roof
far up the Merrimack and lit his fire, watched
his smoke ascending, as he told me, nearer
the North Star than that of any other of his
Majesty's New England subjects. He tooks his
bearings by the stars but squared his logs himself. We still do in America. We swim white
water like the trout in spring: a plunging torrent
where an unknown age rushes upon its destiny.
We have the West before us. We tell our future,
not by calendars of years but by the great
savannahs still unplowed, the centuries of un-
cut forests. As for the rest . . . we fear no
evil but our own and so we meet none. Not
even . . . (An ironic bow.) . . . when the
"Devil" comes to call beneath the elms. I
bid you a good day.

SCRATCH. Good day to you, sir. Till we meet
again.

WEBSTER. That, I fear, will not be soon.

SCRATCH. Oh, do not fear. It will be very soon.
Before the day ends.

WEBSTER. Unhappily, you will not find me here
this evening.

SCRATCH. I will not find you anywhere, Mr.
    Webster. You will find me.
WEBSTER. Perhaps, but not this evening. My
    health was never better.
SCRATCH. You mistake me. I was not thinking
    of an . . . ultimate reunion--not for the mo-
    ment anyway. I had in mind the next resump-
    tion of our little conversation. You interest
    me, Mr. Webster: more and more. I under-
    stand why, when you called on Mr. Jefferson
    at Monticello, he could not get enough of you.
    I quite believe it. (Picking up his hat.) But I
    trespass on your hospitality. (A bow: he be-
    gins to leave the arbor--he turns.) Forgive
    me! One last question. You know Jabez
    Stone?
WEBSTER. Of Cross Corners? In New Hamp-
    shire? Certainly. Who doesn't?
SCRATCH. You think of Mr. Stone as an American?
WEBSTER. American?
SCRATCH. You use the word as one of approbation
    --unusual approbation, if you'll let me say so.
WEBSTER. Then Jabez Stone deserves it. Young-
    est treasurer the Party has ever had in New
    Hampshire or anywhere else in the Union.
SCRATCH. Done well, eh?
WEBSTER. In politics, obviously. In business, too:
    he's made a fortune in the last ten years.
SCRATCH. Not ten years: seven, Mr. Webster--
    seven years precisely lacking . . . just . . .
    one . . . day. . . . But I keep you from your
    numerous concerns, your duties.
WEBSTER. Worse, sir, you keep me from my
    sleep. When a man can't sleep beneath the
    noontime shadows of his garden elms without
    the insults of some passing mountebank he has
    no recourse but his bedroom sofa where he can.

(WEBSTER stumps out.)
SCRATCH. Then all's well. Bravo, Mr. Webster!
    Let's preserve the Union, keep the country
    going . . . get on with business.

(The light fades. We are in:)

Scene 3

Jabez Stone's farm at Cross Corners, New Hampshire. Sunset. A hard-scrabble, New England field. In the middle of the field, among the boulders, and the steeple bush and milkweed, a rusted, one-horse plow lies on its side, its handles twisted against the light. JABEZ, in his city clothes, is standing, staring at the plow. Touching it. SCRATCH comes up behind him.

SCRATCH. Enjoying the sunset, Jabez? Charming moment! . . . that fiery light which leads us to the triumph of the dark . . . beautiful betrayal. (JABEZ neither turns nor speaks.) Engrossed in it, eh? The hour of deception . . . (JABEZ does not move.) And how appropriate! All that blazing red! Couldn't keep away from the old plow, could you, Jabez? Not on what a man might call the . . . happy anniversary. Seven years ago today! (Silence, the reddening sky.) Oh, come, my boy. It's not as bad as that. You've had your seven years--and fat ones. Uninterrupted prosperity! Flowing affluence! (JABEZ turns, looks SCRATCH in the eye.) That's better. Good evening, Jabez. How are you? (Convulsion of silent laughter.) Rarin' to go?

JABEZ (cool and collected). I'm well. Quite well, thank you. What brings you here at this unusual hour?

SCRATCH. What's unusual about it? It happens every day along toward nightfall. Not always as beautiful as this, perhaps, but then not every nightfall is as promising--propitious.

JABEZ. I hadn't thought of it in quite those terms.

SCRATCH (gesture toward the plow). But you <u>had</u>
    thought of it!

JABEZ. I realized, of course, we had a settle-
    ment to make. As a matter of fact, I had it
    down on my calendar.

SCRATCH. Just so you wouldn't forget it in pass-
    ing . . . with everything else you have to think
    about. . . .

JABEZ. The fact is, sir--I have no wish to sound
    inhospitable--the fact is that your call is rath-
    er premature. It isn't time.

SCRATCH. You mean it isn't--shall we say--
    eternity. You're right, of course--quite
    right. You're not . . . due till midnight. (He
    finds a seat on a stump.) Eternity begins at
    twelve! How you will love eternity, Jabez!
    No care for the morrow for there is no mor-
    row. No regret for the vanished past for the
    past never vanishes: it floats along beside
    you on that ceaseless stream like a turd on a
    river. Whenever you look at it it's there,
    watching you, waiting to see what you decide
    to do about it. . . . (Stretching.) Except that
    there is nothing you <u>can</u> do about it. (A deli-
    cious, noisy yawn.) Perfect peace! Perfect
    peace! I mean . . . (Pause.) . . . if only
    you could sleep, it would be perfect. (Pause.)
    But you can't sleep--not with your past beside
    you--floating there.

JABEZ (matter-of-fact). An inviting prospect but
    not, I fear, a prospect meant for me. Not
    this evening.

SCRATCH (closing his eyes). Quite right. Not
    this evening. Not till midnight.

JABEZ. And not at midnight, either. I have im-
    portant business in Concord in the morning.

SCRATCH. It will have to wait . . . (Deep sigh.)
. . . indefinitely.

JABEZ (briskly, reaching into his pockets for
papers--successful young executive in action).
I do not propose that it shall wait, indefinitely
or otherwise. The note may not be due till
midnight but I shall meet it now--repay the
loan at once.

SCRATCH (opening his eyes). What note? What
loan?

JABEZ. The loan you so generously made me
seven years ago. The note which undertook,
upon a specified security, to repay that loan.
(He is counting out banknotes as he talks: he
now offers a little bundle.) Please count them.
You will see I have included interest to the
hour specified. (SCRATCH has not moved.)
And may I take this opportunity to thank you
once again for your great kindness to me.
Without your generous advance of funds I
never should have reached my present--shall
I say--position. It was you, sir, who released
my talents: talents of which I was quite ignorant until we met--until you offered me your
helping hand.

SCRATCH. Keep your money and your gratitude,
my friend. There was no loan: it was a pur-
chase, a price paid. And what you call a note
was not a note. It was a bill of sale promising
delivery on a certain date and at a certain
hour. And as for your sum total, do you
really think my whole investment in this enter-
prise was those few dog-eared, torn, devalued
dollars? Who suggested you for treasurer of
your party in this state? Who told the trustees
of the Franklin Bank they needed a dirt farmer
for their president? (You should have seen

their faces when they found they <u>had</u> one!) No
wonder you were ignorant of your talents,
Jabez. They were never yours.

JABEZ. Naturally if there are further services I
should include I will be happy . . .

SCRATCH. Not services that cash could compen-
sate. Men come to me . . . (Making himself
comfortable.) . . . men come to me as ac-
tors to the make-up table. In life as on the
stage the face precedes the role and few men
make their faces for themselves. One has to
<u>live</u> to do that, and living is too hard for most.
They much prefer my pencil around the mouth
and eyes, and I provide it. For a compensa-
tion. <u>Not</u> in cash. Oh, there are exceptions,
certainly. Take Daniel Webster. A wit in
England says: "No man was ever great as
Daniel Webster looks"--but Mr. Webster
made his face himself . . . or . . . did he?
That's the question, isn't it? Well . . . we'll
see. (Silence: lost in thought.)

JABEZ. Surely there must be some way we can
estimate the total due . . .

SCRATCH (his mind is elsewhere). There is. We
have. You can deliver what you've promised
on the stroke of twelve.

JABEZ. I promised to repay a loan. I stand here
ready to repay it.

SCRATCH (himself again). Did you? Let us consult the document. (He reaches into his inside coat pocket, pulls out the fat, yellow
wallet, opens it: something small and fluttery
and dark flies out. SCRATCH snatches at it
and misses. We hear a small, high, squeak-
ing voice which is nevertheless unmistakably
human, unmistakably Yankee.)

VOICE. Neighbor Stone! Neighbor Stone! Help

me, help me, Neighbor Stone! For God's
sake, help me! (SCRATCH whips out the
red bandanna, catches the tiny creature with
one fling, ties the ends around its leaping
violence.)

JABEZ (the businessman pose gone, his voice
hoarse with terror). That was a human voice!
It called to me!

SCRATCH (thumbing through a wad of papers). I
know. They always shout at first. Most embarrassing.

JABEZ. But I know that voice!

SCRATCH (reading). Scoville, Sherwin, Slater,
Stevens . . .

JABEZ. Stevens! Miser Stevens! That was
Miser Stevens' voice! I'd know it anywhere.

SCRATCH. Here we are: Stone. Everything ship-
shape and apple-pie. (He unfolds a document
and begins to read:) "I, Jabez Stone, of Cross
Corners . . . "

JABEZ. I tell you that was Miser Stevens' voice
and it must be Miser Stevens in your red bandanna and Miser Stevens isn't even . . . dead!

SCRATCH (clearing his throat menacingly). "I,
Jabez Stone . . . "

JABEZ. You can't tell me he's dead. He was just
as spry and mean as a woodchuck Tuesday and
here it is . . .

SCRATCH (the familiar smile). Ah, Jabez, we
don't know, do we? We never know. In the
midst of life we are in . . .

(The tolling of a bell.)

SCRATCH. First Church, I'd say by the sound of
it. They bought a used bell from Second Church
and it turned out just a leetle cracked. The

congregation at Second Church had never even
noticed--so they said. Interdenominational
differences, I suppose.

JABEZ. First Church is Miser Stevens'!

SCRATCH. It . . . (A high, fierce, twanging
whine from the bandanna: the little creature
beating like a June bug against a screen.
JABEZ is staring at it, his face twisted with
horror.) . . . <u>was</u>!

JABEZ. Are they all <u>as</u> . . . small as that?

SCRATCH. As him? Oh, no. They vary. You'll
run fair to middling, Jabez. It's hard to judge
precisely in . . . advance. Except, of course,
in special cases. I mentioned Daniel Webster.
You'd know before you measured with a man
like that. The head alone! Spectacular. Nothing like it since Benjamin Franklin . . . and
he eluded me. . . . Pity! (Pause.) Well,
shall we get on? "I, Jabez Stone, of Cross
Corners . . ."

JABEZ (collapsing). No need to read it. It's a
bill of sale. Delivery at midnight. I know
every word of it by heart. Please! Give me
one more year! Just one!

SCRATCH. We'll make it easy for you, Jabez
. . . easy as we can. (He reaches out, touch-
es JABEZ' head with his hand like a mortician
preparing a corpse.)

JABEZ. I don't want it easy. I just want one
more . . .

SCRATCH. I know. I know. But that's not possible,
is it, Jabez? We have a contract, haven't
we--a bill of sale? A very comprehensive bill
of sale if I do say so: I drafted it myself.

JABEZ. Then I'll break it! I'll get a lawyer and
I'll break it. There never was a contract
drawn a lawyer couldn't break.

SCRATCH. Get a lawyer: you've got one--two, as
a matter of fact. I grant they could be better.

JABEZ. Better . . . I'll get the best. I'll get . . .
Daniel Webster! I'm the Treasurer of the
Party in this state. I have friends. All I have
to do is send for him--he'll come.

SCRATCH. Daniel Webster!

JABEZ. He knows me. Everybody in New Hampshire knows me and Daniel Webster is New
Hampshire born.

SCRATCH. But Daniel Webster is now Secretary.
Secretary of State to Mr. Fillmore!

JABEZ. He's my friend.

SCRATCH. Really? Drop the cares of state for
friendship?

JABEZ. Friendship and a fee. He's always--
short of cash.

SCRATCH. Whereas--how fortunate!--you're not.

JABEZ. He knows I'm good for anything he asks.

SCRATCH. I'm sure he does. But if he's down in
Washington . . .

JABEZ. He isn't. He's next door in Massachusetts.

SCRATCH. Extraordinary! All you have to do is
send? (He studies the fading sky, color of
rusty blood. JABEZ, turning with him, stares
not at the sky but at the plow.) Getting a little
darker, isn't it? I see you're looking at the
old plow, Jabez. Sort of brings things back?
. . . Yep, it's getting darker. Hear those
crickets? Regular kind of clock-tick, isn't it?
That's what they're doing, maybe--counting
time--counting the running out of time. Listen
to them, Jabez! (Silence. We listen to the
crickets--the mechanical, insistent beat.
JABEZ on his knees at SCRATCH'S feet.)

JABEZ. No, no. I didn't mean it. I won't break
the contract--try to. I won't send for anyone

if you'll just help me. One more year, one
more. (Speechless--huddled on the ground.)
Oh, dear God, don't . . . don't . . . (Silence
--the crickets.)

SCRATCH. Maybe, Jabez, you had better send
for Mister Webster.

(JABEZ sags in the dwindling light. The beat of
the crickets is louder and louder.)

CURTAIN

Scene 4

Jabez' farm. Night. The interior of the old barn. A lighted lantern on a nail: another farther back. A few chairs. WEBSTER appears, carpetbag in hand.

WEBSTER. Jabez!

(JABEZ gets up from a dark corner.)

JABEZ. Mr. Webster. . . . Thank God you're here. Thank God.

WEBSTER (looking up and around at the huge beams, and high roof). Your driver, that venerable First Selectman, Mr. Josiah Salter, told me I'd find you in the barn . . . (Putting down his gear.) . . . and here, by Goshas, in the barn you be! What is it, Neighbor Stone?

JABEZ. You mean . . . the barn? I thought we'd be more comfortable here. Wives get nervous when they see a lawyer in the house. Particularly, sir, a famous lawyer.

WEBSTER. And more particularly, Mr. Stone, when they see a lawyer after lawyers' hours-- famous or not. What's wrong? Mutiny among the Whigs? Embezzlement at Franklin Savings?

JABEZ. Oh, nothing like that, sir.

WEBSTER. Well, if it's not the bank and not the party, what is wrong? (His voice has an edge.) Somebody shoot your dog?

JABEZ. No, no.

WEBSTER. Well, then, what did happen? (The door creaks: JABEZ whirls to face it.) Expecting somebody? (JABEZ is silent, motionless, facing the door.) All right. Don't talk till you're

48

a mind to. Maybe something . . . potable *tʃt*
would help. (No answer.) Latin *potabilis*
from *potare*--to drink. (JABEZ turns, his
face blank.) Not to put too fine a point upon it,
Cross Corners applejack is famous.

JABEZ. Ah, yes, forgive me . . . (He goes to find
the applejack.)

WEBSTER. Might even help remind you why you
sent for me to come. (JABEZ is back with the
jug.) Sit down, boy, sit down. I remember
one chill summer evening almost forty years
ago, your grandfather fetched me up a jug of
his Eighteen-ten . . . (JABEZ hands him the
jug and a dingy glass: he rejects the glass.)
I've never learned to drink alone, not even in
Washington--and in Washington you sometimes
have to drink alone . . . if you want a gentle-
man for company. You take the mug, I'll take
the jug. Your health, sir. (A gulp from the
jug, skillfully balanced on the back of his elbow:
pause.) Well? (JABEZ, head down over his
glass.) Take your time, boy. Take your time.
(Another long pull.) I remember teaching your
grandfather a bit of doggerel that evening. He
did not, under ordinary circumstances, care
for song, but a pull or two at the Eighteen-ten
would make a thrush of anybody. It went like
this: (He throws his head back, emitting a deep
tuneless basso-profundo: he is tone deaf.)
When you and I are dead and gone . . . "
(JABEZ gags, coughs.) Hold on, boy! You
have to hold hard when the applejack jerks at
you. So . . . "When you and I . . ." What's
the matter, boy? Ill? You look . . . What is
it, Jabez? Why did you send for me? At midnight!

JABEZ. I'm sorry. I had no choice . . .

WEBSTER. No, no. I was happy to come--happy
    to come . . . and not for your grandfather's
    sake or your father's, but for yours. We re-
    spect and admire you, all of us in New England
    --even the Democrats. But twelve midnight!
    What kind of lawyer's business falls upon that
    hour?

JABEZ. A . . . (Floundering.) . . . mortgage
    case.

WEBSTER. Mortgage case! Foreclosure, you
    mean? At midnight?

JABEZ. Foreclosed.

WEBSTER. Not the home farm, certainly.

JABEZ. The home farm . . . (He looks around him
    at the table, the chairs, the old furniture, as
    though he were seeing them for the first time
    --or the last.)

WEBSTER. Come, come, Jabez. You're one of the
    richest men in the state--the richest maybe
    west of Portsmouth, and Portsmouth smells
    the sea. Pull yourself together, Jabez.

JABEZ. I'm no lawyer, Mr. Webster. All I know
    is . . . well, I've lost . . . everything.

WEBSTER. Listen to me, Jabez. What's all this
    about? Begin at the beginning.

JABEZ. That was seven years ago . . . (Pause.)

WEBSTER. Go on.

JABEZ. Oh, Mr. Webster, I never should have
    sent for you. I can't tell you. My grandfather
    --well, he loved you, Mr. Webster. My father
    honored you. All New England, all the Union,
    honors you. You are the Defender of the Union,
    the Expounder of the Constitution . . .

WEBSTER. I'm afraid you'll have to tell me, Jabez.
    Not that I don't appreciate the sentiments . . .
    (Reaching for the jug.) What happened seven
    years ago?

JABEZ. I was plowing. It was a hot day in a dry
    summer and the hay was in--what hay there was
    that year. I was planning on winter wheat--had
    to have a cash crop somehow with the children
    sick, first one child, then another, and my wife
    as crooked as a scythe snath with the rheumatism.
    I hadn't paid the doctor for a year or anyone
    else but the tax collector and I was late with him.
    So I was plowing--the only piece on the farm you
    can plow--the water-mowing where the brook
    comes in. You have to watch for boulders in that
    meadow and I was watching, thinking of all the
    times I'd plowed the piece before and the times
    my father had plowed it and his father, and all
    at once--well, you can guess. We fetched up
    on a granite boulder must have heaved with the
    frost in the big freeze that winter and the coulter
    broke and the old horse foundered and. . . (His
    voice goes dry in his throat.) Well, I suppose I
    kind of . . . (His voice trails off unconvincingly.)
    . . . cursed . . .
WEBSTER (a bark of a laugh). Who wouldn't!
JABEZ. Except that there was someone passing. I
    could have sworn he wasn't there before and you
    can see the road for a mile from the water-
    mowing. A Boston-looking man in a neat red
    buggy. He dropped the reins and jumped the
    wall as though I'd called him. Exactly as though
    he'd heard me call him. I remember thinking
    he was mighty spry for a Boston man and then
    before I knew it he was there -- talking to me.
    Don't ask me what he said. All I know is, it was
    like a revelation. You know how it is when you
    hear a song and you can't remember the words
    but the moment stays with you, haunts you--
    changes your life? I can't remember the words.
    He took it all in, the broken coulter, the stranded

plow, the foundered horse, the boulders around
in the grass like gravestones, the crooked house,
the barn blown in at the north end, the hills
beyond it--ridge on ridge of wooded hills--and he
wanted to know how a man could live like that
when there were towns to live in, houses with
water laid on by the kitchen sink and coal to heat
with and all the rest of it. You see, I'd always
thought a man did what he had to: stayed put
and did what he had to. That's the way they
brought us up. You did what you had to, best
you could. If the work was hard it was your
work. It never crossed my mind a man could
leave--clear out--live as he wanted to. But
here was this Boston man by the broken plow at
the furrow's end in the hard-scrabble meadow
telling me I could do just that. It was what I
say--a revelation. I saw what a fool I'd been!
(A harsh laugh that ends like a sob.) . . .been!
. . . (Pause.) He offered to help. Said he'd
be back at midnight. With a kind of--advance,
you might say.

WEBSTER. And you signed a note for it? A mortgage note, I think you told me. (JABEZ nods.)
Payable in . . . ?

JABEZ. Seven years: midnight to midnight.

WEBSTER. And the seven years are up? . . .

JABEZ. Tonight. At midnight. Now. O, my God!

WEBSTER (cheerfully). Well, we'll have to ask for
an extension.

JABEZ. You don't understand, Mr. Webster.

WEBSTER. What don't I understand?

(SCRATCH appears behind them, unseen by either.)

WEBSTER. I understand mortgages. This isn't
the first foreclosure in New Hampshire or even

the first in my practice at the bar. (SCRATCH
taps WEBSTER on the shoulder and wheezes a
rusty laugh. WEBSTER, wheeling on him--ex-
ploding.) Oh! Great God in Heaven!

SCRATCH. No, no. You mistake me, Mr. Webster.

WEBSTER. On the contrary. I know how you make
your living. You run a mortgage business . . .
(Heavy irony.) . . . on the side.

SCRATCH. A mortgage business, Mr. Webster?
(A quick look at JABEZ.) Ah, of course, a
mortgage business! In any case we meet again:
I think I . . . prophesied we would. The greatest possible pleasure, Mr. Webster.

WEBSTER. Sit down, will you? (SCRATCH pulls
out his great red handkerchief with a sudden
flourish. JABEZ shrinks. SCRATCH blows
his nose with a resounding ironic blast, sits
down, picks up the jug.)

SCRATCH. I am obliged to you for your presence,
Mr. Webster. It will simplify a sometimes
embarrassing transaction.

WEBSTER. Embarrassing transaction: An attempt-
ed foreclosure of a mortgage is . . . embarrassing?

SCRATCH. Ah, you will have your little pleasant-
ries, Mr. Webster.

WEBSTER. You deny you are here to foreclose a
mortgage?

SCRATCH. Not if you prefer the phrase. (A lip-
licking grin at JABEZ.) Not in the least. Anything he has a mind to call it as long as I get
my rights and judgment is . . . (Lingering
pleasantly over the word.) . . . ex-e-cuted.
(JABEZ huddles into his chair.)

WEBSTER. May I take that to mean you have a
judgment?

SCRATCH. Judgment?

WEBSTER. An adjudication. By a court. Of com-
    petent jurisdiction. Finding the note due, valid,
    and unpaid. Ordering execution on the property.
SCRATCH (savoring the word with a pull at the jug).
    "The property"! (Gagging over the drink.)
    Your client, Mr. Webster, should be indicted
    for his liquor before he is sued for his . . .
    debt!
WEBSTER. Have you, or have you not, an adjudi-
    cation by a court . . .
SCRATCH. . . . . of competent jurisdiction? The
    elegance of your phrases, Mr. Webster. I
    have.
WEBSTER. May I see it?
SCRATCH. Better than that, you may hear it. I,
    Mr. Webster, am the Court of Competent
    Jurisdiction. I will rule . . .
WEBSTER. You will not, sir! Not in Cross Cor-
    ners in New Hampshire in the United States of
    America. In the United States of America a
    litigant does not sit in judgment. Under the
    Constitution . . .
SCRATCH. You and your Constitution, Mr. Webster!
    You'll be telling me next your Constitution has
    supplanted the laws of the universe and your
    people are not as other people.
WEBSTER. It has and they're not. They're a new
    thing under the sun. They're Americans!
SCRATCH. New? (A contemptuous look at JABEZ.)
    Like your client? I can remember a time when
    the new thing under the sun on this continent
    was the red man and his bow. The world was
    much the same then only . . . nobody had
    thought to call it new. A restful moment!
    Well . . . that's gone. . . . And so you want a
    judge and jury?
WEBSTER. Not in the least. You want a judge and

jury.

SCRATCH.   And I won't do.

WEBSTER.   You won't do. No offense intended.

SCRATCH.   And none taken. (Rubbing his chin,
    looking away as a cat looks away from the
    mouse under her claws.) But where in the
    world will I find a judge and jury at this place
    and hour?

WEBSTER.   That, I fear, is your responsibility.

SCRATCH (just a shade too quickly).   My responsi-
    bility?

WEBSTER.   You're the one who needs them.

SCRATCH.   How cogently you put things, Mr.
    Webster. So . . . you leave it to me.

WEBSTER.   If you'll leave it to them. After
    they've heard the evidence, of course, and the
    arguments of counsel.

SCRATCH.   Above all . . . (An ironic bow.) . . .
    the arguments of counsel.

WEBSTER.   Precisely.

SCRATCH.   And that is your one condition? Any
    American judge. Any American jury.

WEBSTER.   Precisely.

SCRATCH.   Then you shall have them, sir. Pre-
    cisely! (He stamps his foot.)

(A throng of white-faced ghastly FIGURES [described
    in subsequent pages] in the dress of other cen-
    turies appears from all corners of the barn.
    JABEZ shrivels in his chair.)

SCRATCH (turning to WEBSTER).   Your judge, sir,
    and your jury! (SCRATCH grins at WEBSTER
    --a long, slow, unsmiling widening grin.)
    Well? . . . (Silence.) You see how it is, Mr.
    Webster.

WEBSTER (looking him full in the face, shoulders

set, feet firm). How it is, and who.

SCRATCH. Not just The Old Scratch any longer,
eh? Not a laughable way of mentioning what no
one mentions laughing. (Pause.) I thought
you'd recognize me once the light was right--
even in General Washington's Republic.

WEBSTER (staring at the jury, turning slowly to
stare at SCRATCH; a silence we can feel--
taste, almost). I owe you . . . apology would
be an inappropriate word but . . .

SCRATCH. I repeat: Your judge and jury!

WEBSTER (facing the jury again). Not mine. I
made, and you accepted, a condition.

SCRATCH. Condition?

WEBSTER. That judge and jury be American.

SCRATCH. American! They are: you have my
word for it.

WEBSTER. They!

SCRATCH. Nothing, sir, was said of live Americans. (A long silence.)

This, sir, is Mr. Justice Hathorne, an American jurist. The best remembered--longest,
anyway--of all American jurists. He presided
at certain famous trials in tne Massachusetts
city of Salem where a number of women--as
you of course remember--were convicted of
. . . witchcraft. They were hanged. No judge,
you will agree, was ever more American than
Mr. Justice Hathorne. Salem . . . the Old
Colony . . .

(HATHORNE stands aside.
A small, dapper man in
Continental uniform advances,
a huge dueling pistol in his
hand.)

Burr! And this is Colonel Aaron Burr.   Once
Vice-President of the United States and . . .
(A glance at WEBSTER.) . . . all but President.
He was indicted for treason later on but not
convicted: he claimed he had merely intended
to make a revolution in Mexico! I think you'll
agree that a Vice-President of the United States
qualifies as an American! It is true of course
that Colonel Burr thought best to leave the
country for a number of years but he returned
--he returned.

> (BURR climbs the ladder to
> the hayloft. THREE MEN move
> forward: the first a tall man in
> the dress of a sea-captain of the
> 1790's; the second a white-faced
> man dressed as a planter of the
> late 1770's; the third a tall man
> in New England professional
> dress of the late eighteenth
> century.)

Wolf! De Wolf! And here . . . here we have
Captain James De Wolf of Rhode Island, the
most famous slave-trader of a state famous for
its trade in slaves. Captain Jim, as he was
affectionately called, was a most enterprising
American. He was elected United States Senator toward the end of his life but disliked the
Washington climate and resigned.

> (DE WOLF joins BURR in the
> loft.)

Lynch! And this is Charles Lynch of Virginia
whose activities as a Justice of the Peace in

that state added a famous word to your interesting vocabulary. Judge Lynch's credentials as
an American are impeccable--a soldier--a
patriot. If he sometimes seemed a little too
enthusiastic in his sentencing of prisoners, his
purposes were admirable. The Virginia As-
sembly, in exonerating him after the Revolution,
specifically stated that his judgments, though
not "strictly warranted by law," were "justifi-
able" because they maintained order in a dan-
gerous time. What could be more fundamen-
tally American than that?

(LYNCH joins BURR and DE WOLF.)

And now! Now! Dr. Benjamin Church of
Massachusetts, the first and only member of
the Revolutionary apparatus in America to have
his family pensioned after his death by the
British Crown! Dr. Church, gentlemen, was
the first American traitor!

(As DR. CHURCH follows
LYNCH up the ladder, a
FIGURE in seventeenth
century dress with blue jowl,
smirking mouth and piously
folded hands moves forward.)

Oh, no! No! There must have been some
misunderstanding. This is Mr. John Webb of
Massachusetts Bay who led the Quaker woman,
Mary Dyer, out onto Boston Common to be
hanged on a damp morning in 1660. But of
course Mr. Webb was not alone. They were
all there from the Governor down. And they
did establish a great American tradition: how

to deal with dissenting opinions. Nevertheless
. . . one has to draw the line at some point.
Well, since you're here, Mr. Webb, up with
you!

> (As WEBB climbs, the rest of
> the jurors crowd in. SCRATCH
> motions them up the ladder.)

Come along! Up with you! This is a distinguished New Yorker--Captain Kidd. A colleague
of his from Ocracoke Island in North Carolina.
An empire-builder from the Northwest Terri-
tories--what he couldn't cut or saw he burned.
A Revolutionary officer who plotted against
General Washington. Nothing is more American
than service in the Revolutionary Army, is it?
Ask the daughters of and the daughters of
daughters and on down . . .

Well, Mr. Webster, are you satisfied?
(Silence.) I asked you: are you satisfied with
judge and jury?
WEBSTER. A judge and jury of the dead and
damned . . .
SCRATCH. American dead and damned!
WEBSTER. . . . to try an action for foreclosure?
SCRATCH. That, I think, was your term, Mr.
Webster. (Silence.) Well . . . we wait on you,
sir. Are you ready to proceed? (A long
silence.)
WEBSTER. Defendant . . . is ready to proceed.
SCRATCH. Oyez! Oyez! Oyez! The Honorable,
the Inferior Court of Common Pleas in the
County of Oyez! Oyez! Oyez! (HATHORNE
enters an old chaise, raps for order.)
HATHORNE. The Court will be in order.

SCRATCH (rising, bowing to the Court, bowing to
the Jury, bowing to WEBSTER). May it please
the Court. This is an action on a debt--not
quite the usual debt but an obligation notwith-
standing--alleged by the plaintiff . . . (Indi-
cating himself with a modest gesture.) . . . to
have been executed by the defendent . . . (A
bow in the direction of JABEZ STONE.) . . .
on the twenty-sixth day of July, eighteen hundred and forty-three, being due and, so to
speak, payable to the plaintiff seven years from
date on the twenty-sixth day of July in the year
eighteen hundred and fifty which is the day just
now, with the passage of midnight . . . (A
vicious sting in his voice.) . . . concluded!

HATHORNE. You may proceed.

SCRATCH. Plaintiff in this action is represented
by himself. Defendant is represented by the
Honorable Daniel Webster . . . (WEBSTER
rises and bows to the Court.) Secretary of
State of the so-called United States of America.
The Secretary takes a serious view of this
litigation. He considers that the vital interests
of what he likes to call the Union are involved,
and nothing--neither time nor space nor bad
roads nor unreasonable hours--has prevented
his presence.

WEBSTER. If the Court please!

HATHORNE. The Court will hear you.

WEBSTER. There is no need for irrelevant and
insulting innuendoes touching the integrity of
the Republic in an action for debt, nor, indeed,
in any other action. The Union stands. It will
continue to stand. Nothing--not all the evil of
the world--can prevent its standing.

SCRATCH. But of course. Of course. I quite
agree. Nothing can destroy the Union--not

even what distinguished counsel eloquently calls
the Evil of the World--nothing at all . . .
(Dropping his voice almost to a whisper.) . . .
except the Union! When the Union has <u>itself</u>
become an evil . . . (Pause.) But counsel for
the defendant is quite right, quite right. As
befits the greatest constitutional lawyer of his
or any other age, he believes in institutions--
particularly the institutions which compose his
Union. He regards them as the wonders of the
world to be preserved at any cost--particularly
at any moral cost . . .

WEBSTER. Your Honor, I protest this . . .

SCRATCH. Not in the least. Not in the least. I
intend nothing offensive, nothing whatever.
Moral costs are the most easily paid of any. A
few tears, a few eloquent and appropriate re-
grets, will do it. Institutions are real. Moral
twinges are--what? Moral twinges!

WEBSTER. May it please the Court . . .

HATHORNE. Come to your point, sir.

WEBSTER. May it please the Court, this is an
action for debt--an action for the collection of
an alleged debt. The United States of America
are not on trial.

SCRATCH. Can we be sure, Mr. Webster? Can
we be sure? You recall your extravagant ad-
miration for your fellow Americans--your be-
lief that no American owes allegiance to a certain . . . power you were kind enough to name.
Suppose we should discover there was one respected American who was capable of precisely
that. Would we not be entitled to assume there
might be others, equally respected, or even
more so, who were equally capable? And if
others, why not many others? Why not all?
Why not your <u>Union</u>?

WEBSTER. If the Court please . . .

SCRATCH. Why not, indeed, that great defender of
the Union who would put the Union first before
everything, even its promises, even the most
solemn of its promises--that great defender of
the Union who has the courage and the honesty
to call the Union what it is?

WEBSTER (the full resounding resonance of his
tremendous voice). If it please the Court . . .

SCRATCH. I will not persist. I will not persist.

HATHORNE (bang of the gavel). Proceed.

SCRATCH. Very well, your Honor. I face, however, a procedural difficulty at the outset. I
wish to put the plaintiff on the stand. Which
means that I must, so to speak, put myself on
the stand as witness and question myself in my
capacity as counsel.

WEBSTER. I have no objection, your Honor.

HATHORNE. Defendant has no objection.

SCRATCH. Thank you, sir. I speak then as counsel
addressing myself as witness. Do you recognize the paper . . . (He draws a folded paper
from his pocket.) . . . I now hand you? I reply in my capacity as witness . . .

WEBSTER. One moment, your Honor. This witness has not been sworn.

SCRATCH. This witness, may it please the Court,
cannot be sworn--has reasons of . . . conscience for declining to be sworn.

WEBSTER. No evidence may be received in any
American court unless the witness has been
sworn to tell the truth, the whole truth and
nothing but the truth.

HATHORNE. Proceed.

WEBSTER. I object.

HATHORNE. Objection overruled.

WEBSTER. I must respectfully persist in my

objection.   No evidence may be received in any
American court . . . (Bang of the gavel.)

HATHORNE. You cannot persist in an objection
after the objection has been overruled. You are
in contempt of this court.

SCRATCH (mildly).   May the witness now reply to
the question?

HATHORNE. Answer the question.

SCRATCH (as counsel).   Do you recognize the paper
in your hand?

SCRATCH (as plaintiff).   I do.

SCRATCH (as counsel).   Describe it.

SCRATCH (as plaintiff).   It is an instrument executed by the defendant, Jabez Stone, and given
me by him seven years ago . . . (Pause.) . . .
yesterday.

SCRATCH (as counsel).   How is this instrument
signed?

SCRATCH (as plaintiff).   Jabez Stone.

SCRATCH. May it please the Court, the plaintiff
submits this document thus described and
authenticated as Exhibit A.

HATHORNE. The document will be marked Plaintiff's Exhibit A.

WEBSTER. I object.

HATHORNE. Objection overruled.

WEBSTER. This, your Honor, is a travesty of
justice.   You have admitted into evidence the
unsworn testimony of a witness who is also a
party to this litigation.   You have overruled my
objection to the admission of this unsworn
testimony and have threatened me with punish-
ment for persisting in the assertion of my
client's most elementary rights.   You are now
offered an exhibit based upon this inadmissible
evidence . . .

SCRATCH. May it please the Court, I think perhaps

I can suggest a means of satisfying the earnest
protests of counsel for the defendant while sav-
ing the Court's time and protecting the interests
of that perfect justice for which your Honor is
revered.

HATHORNE. The Court will hear you.

SCRATCH. There is present in the courtroom, and
immediately available, a witness who can
identify this document and who will have no
slightest objection to being sworn--who will,
indeed, expect it. I refer, of course, to the
defendant.

HATHORNE. Let the defendant take the stand.

WEBSTER. One moment, your Honor. The defendant cannot be compelled to testify against . . .
(He catches himself, pauses.)

SCRATCH. Against himself? Is this, then, a
criminal proceeding, Mr. Webster? I had
understood you to call it an action for a breach
of contract--the foreclosure, I think you said,
of--yes, a mortgage. (WEBSTER sits down.)

HATHORNE. Let the defendant take the stand.
(JABEZ, stumbling, comes forward.) Raise
your right hand. Repeat after me. I do solemnly swear . . .

JABEZ. I do solemnly swear . . .

HATHORNE. That the testimony I am about to give.

JABEZ. That the testimony I am about to give . . .

HATHORNE. Will be the truth, the whole truth and
nothing but the truth . . .

JABEZ. . . . nothing but the truth . . .

So help me . . .

God.

SCRATCH. Your name?

JABEZ. Jabez Stone.

SCRATCH. Residence?

JABEZ. Cross Corners in the State of New Hampshire.

SCRATCH. Occupation?

JABEZ. Farmer.

SCRATCH. Occupation?

JABEZ. Banker. Landed Proprietor. Treasurer
    of the Whig Party in the State of New Hampshire
    . . . (Defiantly.) . . . farmer.

SCRATCH (turning to watch WEBSTER). You are
    an American?

JABEZ. I am.

SCRATCH. Your father was an American?

JABEZ (a note of pride). He was.

SCRATCH. And his father?

JABEZ. His father.

SCRATCH. And his?

JABEZ. His.

SCRATCH. I congratulate you, Mr. Webster. Now,
    Mr. Jabez Stone of Cross Corners in the State
    of New Hampshire, Banker, Landed Proprietor,
    Treasurer of the Whig Party, American and
    descendant of Americans, I show you a docu-
    ment marked Plaintiff's Exhibit A. I ask you if
    you have seen this document before.

JABEZ (a piteous look at WEBSTER). I have.

SCRATCH. I direct your attention to the signature
    at the foot of this document. Do you recognize
    this signature?

JABEZ. I do.

SCRATCH. Whose signature is it? (Silence,
    JABEZ covering his mouth with his hand.)
    Whose signature is it, Mr. Jabez Stone?

JABEZ (barely audible). My signature.

SCRATCH (pleasantly). Your signature. And in
    what--ah--medium is this signature of yours
    inscribed? (No answer.) I ask you, Mr. Jabez
    Stone, in what medium this signature you rec-
    ognize as yours is written. (No answer: the
    jury, stirring, craning.) Would you say ink,

sir? (No answer.) Not ink. In what, then?

JABEZ (very quietly). Blood.

SCRATCH. I did not catch your answer, Mr. Stone.

JABEZ. Blood.

SCRATCH. Very well, Mr. Jabez Stone. You have
   recognized the document marked Plaintiff's
   Exhibit A. You have testified that the signature is yours. Will you now read it·to the jury.

JABEZ. "I, Jabez Stone, of Cross Corners in the
   State of New Hampshire, having received and
   acknowledged an irrevocable promise to supply
   me with all the amenities, comforts and grati-
   fications of life throughout a period of seven
   years of uninterrupted prosperity and continu-
   ing affluence, do hereby undertake and agree
   to deliver . . .

> . . . at the close of business
> . . . being the hour of midnight
> . . . on the last day of the said
>   seventh year . . .

   (His head down: silence.)
   . . . my immortal soul."
   (Silence. WEBSTER staring at JABEZ,
   rising, moving slowly toward him across
   the barn, SCRATCH sidling along behind
   him.)

WEBSTER. Your . . . what?

SCRATCH (whisper). . . . his immortal soul . . .
   (Wheeze of laughter, the jury sniggering,
   cackling, shrieking in derision, a mounting,
   swelling chaos of jeering sound.) That, Mr.
   Webster, is your "mortgage" . . . your "foreclosure" . . . Do you want a "judgment," too?
   (Pause.) On whom? Him? (Silence.) Or on
   your country, maybe? Your bright new world

--which bore him and bears hundreds like him
every day? . . . Not your country? Then,
perhaps, that great defender of your country
who defends now . . . (Contemptuously.) . . .
Jabez Stone! (Silence: the restless jury. Then
JABEZ' frightened, stammering voice.)

JABEZ. Mr. Webster . . . If it please the . . .
may I consult my . . .

SCRATCH. Defendant wishes to consult his lawyer.
Maybe his lawyer should consult one, too.

HATHORNE. The Court will be in brief recess.
(JABEZ, down from the stand, stumbles across
the barn to WEBSTER, huddles beside him.)

JABEZ. You see . . . how it is.

WEBSTER. How it is. And who it is. And what he
wants here.

JABEZ. I'm not worth . . . throw the case up, Mr.
Webster! Let him take me!

WEBSTER. Take you! He's after bigger game.
You're nothing but the fish-head in the mink-
trap, Neighbor Stone!

JABEZ. I know. I know now. He wants you.

WEBSTER. More than me. If he can shame the
country with your shame he'll take the country
--make a butt and byword of our talk of human
decency, of human worth--make fools of all of
us.

JABEZ. You must believe me, Mr. Webster, I
never thought . . . I never meant to get you
into . . . I was . . . frightened! (His face in
his hands.)

WEBSTER. Nothing to be ashamed of, Jabez. I'm
frightened, too. Oh, not the fear of dying: I'm
too old for that . . . too close to it. No, the
fear of losing everything I've loved and lived
for--my whole life--my life's whole work--the
Union . . . the Republic. (Silence, the jurors

creeping from their loft, listening, creeping
nearer, listening.) I've always known--we
all do--that there's evil in the universe. Pur-
poseful evil. Not the opposite of good or the
defect of good but something to which good itself
is an irrelevance, a fantasy--the wish for darkness underneath the love of light. I know that,
Jabez. But to meet it face to face--the contemptuous, derisive laughter! To learn that what it
laughs at is mankind--man's life--man's hope
of life! (Pause.) No, Jabez, I won't pretend
that I'm not frightened.

JABEZ. Oh, Mr. Webster, go while you still can.

WEBSTER. And leave that hope to him! No, Jabez,
there's only one way now to save what he's de-
termined to destroy. (A long pause.) Ever
meet Seth Peterson down at Marshfield? Hired
man? He'd tell you: he tells me! Count by men,
he says, and shame the Devil. He means the
man comes first--whatever man--the last--the
least--because he's last and least. He means
the way to save the country is to save the man.
(Pause.) He's right. I guess there never was
another way. (Pause.) You may be nothing much
to brag of, Jabez, but you're here. By God, I'll
save you.

JABEZ. You can't, Mr. Webster. There's no de-
fense.

WEBSTER. I'll be damned from Hell to Breakfast if
two Americans can't find a way to beat the Devil.

SCRATCH. True, Mr. Webster. Oh, how true.

HATHORNE. The Court will be in . . .

SCRATCH (brutal shout). No! That game is over.
I'll write the rules now and I'll take . . . (Off
across the barn floor like a hawk in a hen-yard.)
. . . what's mine. (He has JABEZ by the arm.
WEBSTER is on his feet.)

WEBSTER. Not yours until you've won your verdict.

SCRATCH. Nonsense! I'll give the verdicts.

WEBSTER. You made yourself a party to this liti-
     gation. You gave me your assurance that the
     jury would decide--and only after it had heard
     the evidence . . .

SCRATCH. You have no evidence!

WEBSTER. . . . and heard the arguments . . .

SCRATCH. There is no argument. Nothing what-
     ever is in issue now. I have him. If this jury
     brought its verdict in for me--as it would bring
     it--what would I have more than I have now?

WEBSTER. If the jury found for you, you'd have the
     scalp of Daniel Webster.

SCRATCH. Ah? (He drops JABEZ, turns to
     WEBSTER: the old, ironic, genial tone.) And
     by the scalp you mean . . . the man?

WEBSTER. The Indians thought so.

SCRATCH. So then we understand each other. If
     the trial continues, something--perhaps one
     might say Mr. Webster's scalp--even Mr.
     Webster--will be at stake? (Long pause.)

WEBSTER. Yes. (They shake hands.)

SCRATCH. Oh, Mr. Webster! (His cat-canary
     smile.) Why, then, we will . . . proceed.

WEBSTER (full voice, pushing JABEZ forward).
     Witness will resume the stand.

SCRATCH. Thank you, Mr. Webster, but we've
     finished with this witness.

WEBSTER. I have the right, I think, to cross-
     examine.

SCRATCH. Cross-examine! He's your client.

WEBSTER. My client but your witness: you put
     him on the stand.

SCRATCH (giving up). Witness will resume the
     stand. (HATHORNE bangs the gavel.)

WEBSTER. Now, Mr. Stone, you have testified

that you signed the instrument here in evidence.

JABEZ. I did.

WEBSTER. That you signed it in blood.

JABEZ. I did.

WEBSTER. In your own blood.

JABEZ. In my own blood.

WEBSTER. You read the document to the jury.

JABEZ. I did.

WEBSTER. Did you read it truly?

JABEZ. I did. Truly.

WEBSTER. It is true then that this document is in
effect a bill of sale of your immortal soul?
Your soul for seven years of affluence--of com-
fort--gratification, I think the word was?

JABEZ (faltering). It is true.

WEBSTER. Now, Mr. Stone, when you retained me
to represent you in this litigation, did you or
did you not inform me of the true nature of this
document? (The jury leans forward, listening.
Even HATHORNE is listening. SCRATCH has
his back to the scene as though it didn't matter.)

JABEZ (an anguished look at WEBSTER; he still
trusts him but . . .). I did not.

WEBSTER. On the contrary, you misled me.

JABEZ. I misled you.

WEBSTER. You permitted me to believe that you
required my services in connection with the
foreclosure of a mortgage?

JABEZ. I did.

WEBSTER. In brief . . . you lied to me.

JABEZ (his eyes fixed piteously on WEBSTER; he
doesn't understand). I lied to you.

WEBSTER. Very well, Mr. Stone. Let us now
have the truth, the whole truth and nothing but
the truth, so help you . . . (The word is like
the thud of an ax.) . . . God! Why did you lie
to me?

JABEZ. I was ashamed of the . . . truth.

WEBSTER. Of having signed that . . . bill of sale?

JABEZ. Of having signed it.

WEBSTER. Then why did you sign it?

JABEZ (in anguish). Because I couldn't bear my
     . . . life.

WEBSTER. What life?

JABEZ. The broken plow. The foundered horse.
     The farm. Those terrible unending winters,
     treacherous springs, the loneliness at dusk,
     the wind at night . . . my wife a girl still and
     grown old--my children sick or dead beneath
     those gravestones in the meadow. The farm. I
     couldn't bear it.

WEBSTER. Your father bore it!

SCRATCH. Really, your Honor. I protest. Why
     does it matter what this witness feels? It is
     totally and eternally immaterial whether Mr.
     Jabez Stone can bear his life. His death, either.

WEBSTER (to HATHORNE). Immaterial, perhaps,
     to counsel for the plaintiff, but not, your Honor,
     to a Court which knows as you do what it is to
     live and die. (Silence--WEBSTER and
     HATHORNE eye to eye.)

HATHORNE (as though to himself). Objection over-
     ruled. (SCRATCH stands staring at HATHORNE.)

WEBSTER. Your father bore it, Mr. Stone. Raised
     four children out of nine. Educated two of
     them. (Brutally.) They bore it . . . but you
     couldn't?

JABEZ. I couldn't.

WEBSTER. You couldn't! So you sold your soul,
     for a mess of . . . gratifications! (A long
     pause: WEBSTER staring at JABEZ STONE: a
     curt, over-the-shoulder word to SCRATCH.)
     Your witness.

SCRATCH. No questions. He admits the transaction.

Confirms the . . . debt is due and payable.
WEBSTER. Due, yes. Payable is for the jury.
SCRATCH. What do you mean? You yourself have
told your client that he sold his soul. . . .
Something, you <u>once</u> believed, that no <u>American</u>
would do!
WEBSTER. Something one American, alas, has
done.
SCRATCH. <u>One</u> American! Multitudes of them.
Multitud<u>e</u>s! There was even one who sold his
<u>country's</u> soul!

Ever hear of that one, Mr. Webster? Sold it
for peace, he said . . . to preserve the Union!
Took back his country's promise to mankind
for a few years' peace--for a spell of prosperity. <u>You</u> remember that one, don't you?

Oh, to be sure, it was a childish promise, a
ridiculous promise, the kind of promise men
believed in back in those American woods--rat-
tle of idiot words like sleet on the oak leaves
--like gabble of geese in the autumn sky--like
a loon on a lake.

All men had a right to liberty!
　　　　　　　　　　Men!
　　　　　　　　　　　　Liberty!

Anyway you took it back. You were an honest
man and sensible and you took it back:

<u>All</u> men had a right to liberty, yes, but if a
<u>black</u> tried to use it he was still a slave--worse
<u>than</u> a slave--a <u>fugitive</u> slave. You returned
him to . . . <u>servitude</u>. It was all in the Constitution, you <u>said</u>, and besides, it would keep

the peace, preserve the Union.

That was what you told the country, Mr. Webster, and it worked. It preserved the Union . . . for a little . . . (Pause.) Nevertheless there was one American who sold his country's soul.

I wonder, Mr. Webster, if you think he sold his own? We'd welcome him if he did. (To the jury.) Wouldn't we, gentlemen? (Pause.) I didn't catch your answer, Mr. Webster. Did he sell his soul? (Silence.) Or is that what you mean? Is that perhaps the question for the jury? (The jury gathering silently around WEBSTER--a long silence.)

WEBSTER. The question for the jury, sir? The question for the jury? The question for the jury is what it always has been from the first beginnings of the dream of human justice.

The question for the jury is the question of imperfect man: whether a man must perish because he has deserved to perish . . . Whether a nation, because it has deserved to fall, must fall. Whether fallible, imperfect, erring man must pay for error by the letter of the law, the judge's cold adjudication, the mathematics of the fault, or by that other judgment of the fallible. imperfect, erring human heart.

That, sir, is the question for the jury . . .

And juries know the answer. Courts may state the law and counsel argue but the jury knows. The court rules that a contract, duly executed, shall be binding on the parties. The jury sees the contract, finds it duly executed. But there

is something else . . . the jury sees: a hungry
farm, a foundered plow-horse struggling in a
furrow, a man beside the struggling horse.

It hears . . . (Turning, lifting his face to the
jury.) a man's voice . . . (Silence.) . . .
cursing God.

The jury tastes those raging words in its own
mouth. It feels the sweating horse against its
fingers. It is there! (Pause.) I trust my
client's life to you. Not . . . (A bleak smile.)
. . . to your pity! I cannot ask for pity and you
have none. Not to your pity. To your indignation. To your rage. You are the jury and you
know! You know what life is, the injustice of it.
You know the huge injustice of our death.

> (SCRATCH chuckles: WEBSTER
> lifts his arm, levels it at
> SCRATCH.)

You know what laughs at human suffering: it
laughed at you. You know the trap that closed
on Jabez Stone: the same trap closed on you,
each one of you. You know it all. Why Jabez
Stone cursed God. You yourselves have cursed
God--every one of you.

Gentlemen, I have one word still to say. (Pause.)
Counsel for the plaintiff has suggested to you that
something more than Jabez Stone is here on
trial. (Pause.) That I am . . . and my country
which . . . is also yours. He thinks that if he
tangles them all three together in a common
case, so that a verdict for the one must be a
verdict for the others, you will not find for

Jabez Stone because you will not wish to find
for me--or for your country. He thinks, because you're dead and damned, you hate your
country and all those who serve her.

Well, gentlemen . . . I challenge that assumption.

There may be much in our Republic which en-
rages you--I speak to you, sir, Colonel Burr.
There may be much. But honest indignation is
not hate. It scorns the false to find the true
and so it learns to love the true. As you have
learned, in death, to love your country. Not,
Colonel Burr, as you once thought, because
she offered you an empire for your glory. Not,
as you thought, Captain Jim, because you made
a fortune from her shame. Not because God
had given her to you--to _your_ church and no
other, Mr. Webb, as you believed in Boston
Common. Not, Mr. Lynch, because her lash
kept order and you swung the lash. Not, as
every one of you once dreamed, because her
new-found lands would make your fortunes.

Not even, as I told the Senate four months and
nineteen days ago, because her destiny is great-
ness--because her trade will sweep the oceans
and her power lead the world. I was as wrong
as any of you and more wrong. You learned the
truth before me. Your indignation taught you
in the night of Hell. Learning there to hate all
human suffering you learned to love what hopes,
however faintly, for an end of suffering--a
second morning of mankind. (Pause.) I trust
your indignation, gentlemen.

I trust your rage to find for Jabez Stone--and
not in spite of the Republic but because of it.
You will not take the life of Jabez Stone to be
revenged upon your country. Rather, you will
save his life to show your country what she ought
to be--the one place on this sorry earth where
human misery will not be punished with more
misery--where even human folly can have hope.
You understand this, dead and damned, as no
smug jury of the righteous ever could.   (He
pauses, stoops a little, seems to look inward.)
So much, then, for my country.

As for me, what Counsel for the Plaintiff tells
you is quite true, as is so much . . .
          (A wry bow to SCRATCH.)
                              alas . . .
                                   of what . . .

he's said to you.   I am on trial here.   And not
only here but everywhere throughout New England.
And not on trial alone but tried--convicted--
sentenced.   There is no need for you to find
against me: the world has found against me,
my friends have found against me, even my
hired man who is my wisest friend.   The best
in Boston say I showed myself four months ago
to have no care for human things,   and least of
all for human freedom, but only for the letter
of the law, the letter of the Constitution.   "Liberty," they say, "on Webster's lips is like the
words of love upon a whore's." (Pause.)

Gentlemen, I am an old man at my life's end
and at the end dishonored. I know well what my
place in history will be if Massachusetts writes
the histories--and she will. I shall be called a

traitor, not to my country only but mankind; a cold, unfeeling, devious politician who set the dogs upon the fugitives, the fleeing slaves-- hunted them down along the northward rivers.

Well, we are damned together, gentlemen--and, no doubt, for cause. Thirteen damned men in a windy barn! We'd help each other if we could, from common sympathy. Alas, there's nothing you can do for me: nothing but one thing--set the record straight . . . prove that on this night, the man came first before the letter of the law. Prove that thirteen damned men, in this windy barn, fought for the freedom of a frightened human creature as those who talk so loud of freedom never fight--snatched him from the jaws themselves of Hell!

Give me Jabez Stone to prove it and lift the hope of desperate humanity beyond the reach of Hell --the reach of Heaven--even beyond the reach of those who think themselves the surrogates of Heaven . . . those priests of human freedom who would burn the country down to make men free . . . ultimate hypocrites!

      (Silence, a long silence:
      he is near exhaustion.)

Years ago, gentlemen, answering the first secessionists in Carolina, I gave the Senate a brief text by which to hope. "Liberty," I said, "and Union." I see now that I made it better than I knew: Liberty cannot endure without the Union. Union has no meaning without liberty. And liberty is one by one--one man--each man-- however weak, however desperate.

Give me Jabez Stone! (A long pause, head
down.) Defendant rests.

SCRATCH. Thank you, Mr. Webster. An eloquent
address. Remarkable how many eloquent ad-
dresses are delivered when the cause is lost and
evidence is lacking. Now, your Honor, time
presses, as you'll see by that faint window.
One never knows with light like that when some
ambitious cockerel will choose to tell the universe he's up and so the sun must follow. Once
that happens, gentlemen like those that grace
this jury must be . . . elsewhere. (Raising his
voice.) May it please the Court! The parties
rest. Perhaps the jury should withdraw to . . .
weigh its verdict!

HATHORNE. The jury will withdraw. (The jury
leaves.)

SCRATCH. Now, Mr. Stone, if you will take that
chair. Make yourself as comfortable as possible.
Unfortunately--not my doing, I assure you--not
at all--I'd have it otherwise and easier if I
could--unfortunately, the last human breath is
like the first--painful. At birth, I have been
told, men choke and scream in protest. I can
understand that. At the end they merely . . .
choke. (He arranges JABEZ' position in the
chair.) There! That's better, isn't it? We'll
bring you through as easily as we can. (He
draws his red bandanna over JABEZ' head.)
Now! Breathe as I direct you. Inhale, exhale.
Deeply. Always deeply.

(The jury returns.)

DE WOLF. If your Honor please, the jury has
· considered.

HATHORNE. How finds the jury?

DE WOLF. The jury finds for the . . . defendant.

SCRATCH. You have mis-spoken, sir. You said
    . . . defendant. (A threatening step forward.)

DE WOLF (the jury gathering behind him, their
    heads high, terrified but brave). The jury
    finds for the defendant and I so say.

WEBSTER (slowly, to jury). Thank you . . . (Long
    pause.) Gentlemen!

(The high, bright silver shriek of a cock. The chain
    of the door breaks. The huge door opens. The
    room floods with sunlight. The judge and jury
    vanish into the cracks and crevices of the barn.
    WEBSTER crosses slowly to JABEZ, takes the
    contract from JABEZ' hand, tears it to pieces.)

WEBSTER. Well, Neighbor Stone, looks like morn-
    ing. With your permission, sir, I'll try the
    brook. Perhaps a gaudy hackle underneath those
    alders . . . You know I can't abide to be indoors
    when once there's light along the woodlots. I
    trust you will forgive an old man's crotchets.
    (To SCRATCH.) And you, sir--shall we meet
    at breakfast? Breakfast at Cross Corners has
    no equal in New England . . . unless you'll grant
    me Marshfield. Jabez! I'll be back by seven.
    Three fried eggs and seven strips of that Cross
    Corners bacon to adorn my trout. Coffee. (He
    turns towards the open door.) Ah, the morning!
    The glory of the new-world morning! Untouched,
    you'd say . . . (A grin at SCRATCH.) . . .
    since the Creation!

SCRATCH. Untouched! Examine it more closely,
    my exuberant friend. Bite the apple. Suck the
    plum. You'll learn a thing or two about your
    bright new world.

WEBSTER (he turns back from the door). Oh, I've
     learned a thing or two. I've learned that in
     America a man can face the Devil--even shake
     his hand--and still not lose his soul.

SCRATCH. Your soul! You've lost the presidency,
     Mr. Webster.

WEBSTER. I thought of that when you revealed the
     truth about my client and I decided to defend
     him, shame and all. As I'll defend my country,
     shame and all . . . my young republic, west-
     ward of the world . . . with her dark flaw upon
     her!

SCRATCH. Of course! Your country right or
     wrong! We've seen your kind in Hell, sir:
     we'll see you.

WEBSTER. Not my country right or wrong. My
     country with her wrong to right.

SCRATCH. By civil war!

WEBSTER. No. By reason. And in peace.

SCRATCH. I trust you will forgive me, Mr.Webster.
     I suffer from a form of double vision which
     imposes sometimes on the present what is not
     present--yet. It afflicts me now. I see a
     wounded army straggling over red clay roads.
     I hear a voice shout. I hear too what is shouted.
     "The Union forever! Hurrah, boys, hurrah!"
     . . . and silence . . . and no answer . . . and
     the guns.

WEBSTER. Then you hear badly, Scratch, Old
     Scratch! I hear the future shouting, too. It
     says: Liberty and Union, one and inseparable,
     now and forever! And the whole sky answers it.
     (He moves to the place where we first saw him
     at the beginning of the play . . .) . . . now and
     forever . . . (Silence.)

SCRATCH. Liberty and Union! Chalk and cheese!
     Poor, deluded, cracked old man! What's

liberty? A daydream! Some frontier idiot in the
frozen woods watching the wild geese overhead
and dreaming he can follow them! That's liberty
--all the liberty there'll ever be. Union's the
opposite--the fenced-in barnyard; docile cattle,
shoulder to shoulder in the trampled mud. That's
Union--the slow, silent herd. That's real, the
other's fantasy. Put the two together and you
get . . . a fraud! Like your Republic! (Silence
--he moves to the place where we first saw him
at the beginning of the play.) You get war.

JABEZ (he has risen from his chair and stands at
the place where he was at the beginning of the
play; he speaks to the audience). Mr. Webster
believes in the Republic and that's enough for
me. He believes that's what men are . . . (He
is out of his depth and knows it.) . . . bullocks
in a herd and . . . well . . . (Weakly.) a dream
of birds . . .

SCRATCH. You know, Jabez, I don't really care
for you. It's only conscience keeps me laboring
for your soul.

JABEZ (floundering and therefore bold). A dream
of birds. He believes in it and I believe in it.

SCRATCH. You! You'd believe anything--even
that you've seen the last of me.

JABEZ. Maybe I have. It's morning. I'm still
. . . here.

(Motionlessness. Silence.)

THE END

PROPERTIES

GENERAL

OLD BARN: Interior of barn: wall, huge door, window above door, hayloft with ladder leading to it. Old furniture, discarded farm machinery (pre-Civil War), old flag, bust of George Washington, figurehead of ship. <u>Scene Four:</u> Two lighted lanterns hung on nails, several chairs, jug of apple-jack and a glass.

KITCHEN: Large table with big pine chair at head, several chairs placed around table, lanterns. Table is set for breakfast (plates, silverware, etc.) with large pot of coffee, pint pitchers of cream, butter piled on plates, bowls of summer flowers.

BACK YARD: Webster's chair, elm trees.

FIELD: Boulder, steeple bush, milkweed, stump, rusted one-horse plow.

PERSONAL

SCRATCH: Large sack, large red handkerchief, fat yellow leather wallet, wad of papers, folded document.

HIRED GIRL: Spoons, plates, napkins, cups; platters of steak, eggs, bacon, pie.

PETERSON: Newspaper clipping.

JABEZ: Papers, banknotes.

WEBSTER: Carpetbag.

BURR: Dueling pistol.

HATHORNE: Gavel.